Just So

Also by Alan Watts

The Spirit of Zen (1936)

The Legacy of Asia and Western Man (1937)

The Meaning of Happiness (1940)

The Theologica Mystica of St. Dionysius (1944)
(translation)

Behold the Spirit (1948)

Easter: Its Story and Meaning (1950)

The Supreme Identity (1950)

*The Wisdom of Insecurity: A Message
for an Age of Anxiety (1951)*

Myth and Ritual in Christianity (1953)

The Way of Zen (1957)

Nature, Man, and Woman (1958)

*"This Is It" and Other Essays on Zen
and Spiritual Experience* (1960)

Psychotherapy East and West (1961)

*The Joyous Cosmology:
Adventures in the Chemistry of Consciousness* (1962)

The Two Hands of God: The Myths of Polarity (1963)

Beyond Theology: The Art of Godmanship (1964)

*The Book: On the Taboo Against
Knowing Who You Are* (1966)

Nonsense (1967)

*Does It Matter? Essays on
Man's Relation to Materiality* (1970)

Erotic Spirituality: The Vision of Konarak (1971)

The Art of Contemplation (1972)

In My Own Way: An Autobiography 1915–1965 (1972)

*Cloud-Hidden, Whereabouts Unknown:
A Mountain Journal* (1973)

Posthumous Publications

Tao: The Watercourse Way (unfinished at the time
of his death in 1973, published in 1975)

The Essence of Alan Watts (1974)

Essential Alan Watts (1976)

*Uncarved Block, Unbleached Silk:
The Mystery of Life* (1978)

Om: Creative Meditations (1979)

Play to Live (1982)

*Way of Liberation: Essays and Lectures
on the Transformation of the Self* (1983)

Out of the Trap (1985)

Diamond Web (1986)

The Early Writings of Alan Watts (1987)

*The Modern Mystic: A New Collection
of Early Writings* (1990)

Talking Zen (1994)

Become Who You Are (1995)

Buddhism: The Religion of No-Religion (1995)

The Philosophies of Asia (1995)

The Tao of Philosophy (1995)

Myth and Religion (1996)

Taoism: Way Beyond Seeking (1997)

Zen and the Beat Way (1997)

Culture of Counterculture (1998)

*Eastern Wisdom: What Is Zen? What Is Tao?
An Introduction to Meditation* (2000)

*Eastern Wisdom, Modern Life: Collected Talks:
1960–1969* (2006)

*Out of Your Mind: Tricksters, Interdependence,
and the Cosmic Game of Hide-and-Seek* (2017)

Just So

Money, Materialism, and the
Ineffable, Intelligent Universe

Alan Watts

sounds true
BOULDER, COLORADO

Sounds True
Boulder, CO 80306

Published 2020

Cover design by Jennifer Miles
Book design by Beth Skelley

Printed in Canada

Library of Congress Cataloging-in-Publication Data

Names: Watts, Alan, 1915-1973, author.
Title: Just so : money, materialism, and the ineffable, intelligent universe /
    Alan Watts.
Description: Boulder, CO : Sounds True, 2020. | Includes bibliographical
    references.
Identifiers: LCCN 2019020418 (print) | LCCN 2019981059 (ebook) |
    ISBN 9781683642947 (paperback) | ISBN 9781683642954 (ebook)
Subjects: LCSH: Conduct of life. | Wealth. | Materialism. | Technology.
Classification: LCC BJ1581.2 .W364 2020 (print) | LCC BJ1581.2 (ebook)
    | DDC 191—dc23
LC record available at https://lccn.loc.gov/2019020418
LC ebook record available at https://lccn.loc.gov/2019981059

10 9 8 7 6 5 4 3 2 1

Contents

About This Book

The edited talks used in *Just So* were originally recorded decades ago on the ferryboat SS *Vallejo*, the home and studio of Alan Watts, which was docked at the north end of Sausalito, California. His son, Mark, had been recording Watts's public lectures across the United States for years and in 1972 began to compile audio college courses based on these recordings. The first of these audio courses were offered on cassette, which at the time allowed for widespread mobile listening in cars and on portable decks.

After Watts passed away in 1973, Mark continued to develop courses based on his father's work and established the Alan Watts Electronic University out of a cabin on the slopes of Mount Tamalpais in Marin County. Mark also created the *Love of Wisdom* radio series founded on his father's talks, repurposed much of Watts's material in digital media, produced *Why Not Now?* (a retro-media collage about his father's life), and continues to work on a number of forthcoming archival and creative projects. Like *Out of Your Mind* (Sounds True, 2017), *Just So* is an editorial collaboration with Robert Lee.

1

Going
With

As Westerners, we're accustomed to using a certain kind of language as well as a certain kind of logic that comes with that language. To begin with, we're used to thinking of the world and describing it in terms of particles—an assortment of particles bouncing around in some orderly fashion, much as in the game of billiards. We think about our psychology, our bodies, and our relationships to the outside world in the billiard-like terms of Newtonian mechanics, which actually goes back to some of the atomic theories of people like Democritus—a pre-Socratic philosopher who lived nearly 2,500 years ago.

Accordingly, we need to begin with some idea about the history of these atomic theories. The very notion of atoms has fascinated people for the longest time. What's all this stuff made of? What comprises the world, the human body?

Well, there's one straightforward way to find out what's inside a particular structure or organism, and that's to take a knife and chop the thing in two. Of course, when you do that, you now have two pieces of the thing you started out with, but you also discover in the process that the interior of that particular thing has its own structure. And in the example of the human body, that particular structure involves bones, tissues, organs, and so on.

This discovery invites further inquiry in turn. What, then, are organs made of? Chopping them up reveals yet more structures and even smaller components, which encourages us to keep chopping, and we keep doing that until we've got pieces that are so small they're the same width as the edge of our knife. So we can't cut or break these pieces down until someone invents a better knife, one with an even keener edge.

Through this process, we eventually discover—or believe we discover—pieces so tiny that they can no longer be reduced to smaller components. For the longest time, these fundamental components were called atoms. In Greek, the word for "indivisible" is *atomas*, which we can divide into the components *a* ("non") and *temnein* ("to cut"). So an atom was proposed to be the smallest particle of matter that could no longer be sliced down into smaller particles. This was the originating idea for Democritus's atomism, which conceives that the world is built up in the same sort of way that a house is constructed of bricks or stones, with smaller fragments contributing to a larger whole. In other words, the world itself is a composite of fundamental particles.

For some reason, these fundamental particles were conceived of as little balls, probably because balls can prove somewhat difficult to cut. Try slicing a billiard ball with a sword sometime—it will mostly likely jump off to one side of the cut. Actually, I should say that the early notions of atoms asserted that atoms of liquid substances resembled balls. Atoms of solids, on the other hand, were envisioned as cubes because cubes stack together rather firmly. Liquids slosh around all over the place, so they must have been spherical. Furthermore, if I recall correctly, the atoms that were said to make up fire were supposedly shaped like pyramids. I can't remember what air atoms were supposed to look like—maybe sausages or something like that.

Fundamentally, these are the underlying ideas that make up Western thought. Even today, we think of atoms and subatomic particles in the same way we envision larger planetary systems. These impossibly small components move around and around each other and occasionally bang into and off each other in a predictable fashion, as I said before—just as one finds in the game of billiards.

Needless to say, the Newtonian billiard-based model won't do anymore. You can't simply explain the movement of atoms as a series of sequential collisions. Things just don't behave that way, and the reason they don't behave that way is because they are not separate from each other in the first place—you can identify different waves, but it's still just one ocean waving. And even when you single out one individual wave, you'll never find a crest without a trough. Half waves don't appear in nature. In the same way, you never find solids without space or space without solids—they are different aspects of each other. Positive and negative poles are always found together, too, and an electric current requires both in order to flow. Just so, individuals and their environments exist in polar relationship as different aspects of a single energy.

It isn't correct to say that we're all one huge being, either. Existence is composed of being and nonbeing, solid and space, crest and trough. Fundamentally, the energy of the world is vibratory—on and off—and you'll never find one without the other. "To be or not to be" is certainly not the question because *to be* implies *not to be*, just as *not to be* implies *to be*.

Theology and the Laws of Nature

The language and logic we use about the world—especially when it comes to the laws of nature—also come from our theology. The theology that most of us inherited and grew up with is decidedly Judeo-Christian, which means that the image of the universe we have acquired is basically monarchical. Our way of thinking comes from a culture that conceives of the world as a construct evoked out of nothingness by the commandment of a celestial king.

I don't suppose that those of you reading this who happen to be Christians and Jews still hold to some naive idea of God. That being said, the main thing that I want to get across here is that most of our ideas of God—our images, symbols, and mythological forms we use to describe the divine—have an extremely powerful influence on our feelings and on the ways we behave.

For example, when I was a child, I was a member of the Church of England. In the Church of England, it's quite obvious—from an emotional point of view as distinct from an intellectual point of view—that God stands behind the king of England. And it was perfectly clear, especially as a small boy, that the king and the archbishop of Canterbury and the whole hierarchy of lords, ladies, and officials descending from them were somehow intimately involved with the hierarchy of heaven.

At morning prayer, to which we went every Sunday, the minister would pray, "O Almighty Father, High and Mighty King of Kings, Lord of Lords, the Only Ruler of Princes who dost from thy throne behold all the dwellers upon earth, most heartily we beseech thee with thy favor to behold our most gracious sovereign Lord King George . . ." et cetera. And all the clergy in their robes proceeded in a courtly manner to the altar—which is a kind of earthly symbol of the throne of heaven—where they offered this petition with all proper humility.

You take such things for granted when you're brought up in that kind of environment. It's just the natural attitude you have toward God. But imagine how strange this all would seem to someone from a culture where God is not conceived in the image of kingship. What's with all of this bowing and scraping going on before the throne?

Well, in our history, thrones are essentially places of terror because anybody who rules by force is fundamentally terrified. That's why monarchs are surrounded with all of these protections and why they have to be addressed in the correct language.

If you enter an ordinary court of law in the United States today, you're expected to behave within the confines of strict etiquette. You can't laugh in court, or else the judge will bang the gavel and threaten you with contempt and all sorts of dire punishments. Everyone is required to be serious. It's like that at parades, too, where the marines line up with grim expressions and salute the flag, which is apparently serious business.

So kings are afraid of laughter and also of being attacked. That's why everybody must kneel down before them, because kneeling and prostrating puts you at a disadvantage. The king stands or sits above you on the throne, bodyguards arranged to either side. We see this play out in the Church today—the bishop on his throne, flanked on either side by his attendant canons and clergy. The Catholic cathedrals of old were called *basilica*, meaning "royal palace" in Latin, from the Greek *basileus*—"king."

{ *Jehovah is just a polite way*
of saying what can't be said. }

Some of the ways in which God is addressed in the Bible—for example, King of Kings or Lord of Lords—are actually borrowed from the names that were employed for Persian emperors. Furthermore, certain rites that have become associated with Christianity are, in fact, reflections of the great autocratic monarchs of ancient times: the Cyruses of Persia, pharaohs of Egypt, and Babylonian kings like Hammurabi. In this way, people began to conceive of the universe as being ruled in the same political pattern. Hammurabi, in particular—and Moses after him—were the supposed wise patriarchs who laid down the rules by divine decree. They were the ones who said, "Now, this is the way it's going to be. Since you can't agree among yourselves, I'm here to tell you how everybody is supposed to behave. And since I'm the toughest guy around here, and I've got all of these brothers who are pretty tough themselves, we're going to say that this is the new law, see? And now everybody has to obey." And they did.

So this is how we historically arrived at this idea that there are *laws* to nature, as if somebody powerful told nature what to do. "And God said, 'Let there be light,' and there was light. And God saw the light, and it was good, and God divided the light from the darkness." It was a command—a commandment to nature from God himself. The quest for the laws of nature is akin to the quest for the true understanding of the word of God, who created the universe simply by the breath of his mouth. "In the beginning was the Word, and the Word was with God, and the Word was God." But what is the word?

If we knew the word of God, we could perform incredible magic. That's why the name of God in the Bible is not to be uttered except once a year, and only then by the high priest in the Holy of Holies. We don't really know how the name was pronounced—it's all mixed up in translation—so we just have a combination of consonants and vowels that we name *Jehovah*. But Jehovah is just a polite way of saying what can't be said. If you actually know the name of God, you have unbelievable power—the power of God.

This is why all ancient forms of magic are based on knowing the names of God. In Islam they say that God has a hundred names but that people only know ninety-nine of them. The camel is supposed to know that last name, which is why camels go around looking so snooty all the time. I've also heard that people of some so-called primitive tribes are loath to reveal their own names because when someone knows your true name, it means they can utter it and have power over you.

This might sound like a silly idea, but it is exactly how it's been with science. Western science is essentially the knowledge of names, and that itself is a kind of magic. Understanding the laws of nature means understanding the words underneath phenomena, which means you can change those phenomena, and that's definitely magic. The exception here is that scientists have actually become rather sophisticated of late, having realized that the word comes after the event itself. In other words, "in the beginning" *wasn't* the word. Unless you consider the Hindu idea that speech is the basis of creation, but by speech they mean vibration—sound, you see? They say that if you really get into what sound is about, you'll understand the whole mystery of things because the whole mystery of things is essentially vibrating energy—on and off, it's as simple as that. Life and death—life is *on*, death is *off*. And you have to have one to have the other. In this way, they say that the roots you find in Sanskrit are not simply the building blocks of the language—they're the very roots of life.

Thinking Makes It So

In this way, you create the *world* by the *word*. You might not be very conscious of doing so, but it's the way you think that determines your basic reactions to everything you encounter and perceive. As Hamlet says to Rosencrantz and Guildenstern, "For there is nothing either good or bad, but thinking makes it so."

Thinking makes it so, and thinking is talking to yourself inside your head. This is how we build up all sorts of weird notions—for example, when we say things like "Well, one day I'll have to die." Why *have to* die? What do we mean by such a thing? What's the emotional content involved with saying that? In this case, it means that death is going to be imposed on me against my will. This particular sentence—"I'll have to die"—is stated passively, as if one day I will be compelled to do so. But I can't be compelled to die unless I'm fighting against it. But what if I wanted to die? Suppose I committed suicide?

We could look at dying another way entirely. We could, instead, say something like "Well, one day I'll get a disease and die as a result of it." That's active. I'm taking part. Getting a disease in this case is something I do, just as much as taking a walk. But we somehow get this weird notion that death is not supposed to happen; we have our thoughts arranged so that we believe that a disease is something we're not supposed to get. Even plain old age is something we ought not do. You're supposed to just go on.

We've got this hang-up about life being divided into two parts: There are the things we do, and then there are the things that happen to us. For this reason, Westerners have a habit of misunderstanding karma and talk about it as if the awful things that happen to a person are the punishment for bad behaviors enacted in some previous life. That's nonsense. Karma simply means *your doing* or *your action*—it's not some type of punishment passively received from an external source. If you were to understand karma and recognize that whatever happens to you is actually your own doing, then it's never bad karma. It's only truly bad karma if you refuse to admit that it's your own doing—for example, if you blame someone or something else for it or speak of karma as if it is something mysteriously happening to you.

So what does this have to do with our Western notions of the laws of nature? Consider that we have been told that God's commandment is the foundation for everything that happens in the world today. At the same time, contemporary science promotes an entirely new idea about the laws of nature, which asserts that these so-called laws are not things that exist in any real sense. You can clearly see that the universe is doing all of this stuff, but what we have been calling *laws* depends entirely on these human brains that are oriented to make sense of it all.

One of the ways we make sense of it all is by the principle of regularity—something quite important to us. Take a clock, for example. A clock ticks regularly; the world does not. Inconveniently enough, the earth does not go around the sun neatly in a precise 360 days—a fact that has irritated calendar makers throughout the ages. How do you make a rational calendar? You can't. There isn't an obvious solution because the rotation of the earth upon its own axis does not neatly synchronize with its rotation around the sun, so there's always something a little odd and wobbly about it.

But that doesn't stop us from superimposing the ideal figure of a circle with its 360 degrees over a rather odd elliptical path. Doing so is the same thing as placing a ruler upon a piece of wood and saying, "This piece of wood can be cut to twelve inches." Now, inches are not something that exists in the wood itself. Inches are simply a method—a technique—that some humans invented for measuring things. And so we can cut a piece of cloth or a trunk of a tree to so many feet. Originally, we compared that tree trunk with our bodies—this trunk is so many of our feet long or so many spans if we use our hands. And the inch is, of course, roughly the length of one of our finger joints.

Our bodies typically have a regular shape to them—five fingers on a hand, ten toes all together—and by stretching ourselves out and applying that regularity to nature, we believed we could measure it.

This is precisely the type of measurement we find when it comes to our laws of nature. A law of nature is exactly the same kind of thing as a ruler—it's a way of thinking that enables us to control our environment by observing what we perceive as regularities, applying a calculus, and betting that the environment will be just as regular next time. And the odds are that it may be. If the environment does something once in a particular way, it's likely to do it again in a similar fashion, and that's how people were first able to predict things such as solar eclipses and the phases of the moon. They measured them—counting how often such and such a thing did this and how often such and such a thing did that.

What happens if you can make these kinds of predictions? To other people who haven't yet figured it out, it seems like magic. It can even appear as if nature itself is obeying your command. All you have to do is announce that the moon is going to change at a particular time, say, at so many days from now it's going to take a crescent shape. And the people will think you're actually making it happen. In this way, some predictions establish people in privileged positions, simply because they were able to foretell change.

This is what I'm getting at when I say that the laws of nature are established by the human network. We project the lines of celestial latitude and longitude on the sky, but those lines don't actually exist in the heavens—they're simply a way for us to measure the positions of the stars, which are upon closer examination scattered all over the place in a way that would otherwise be somewhat confusing. Just try to remember that mess up there and figure it out! So some clever someone decided to overlay a spherical network on the sky in accordance with the principle of a circle—360 degrees. That makes a nice, regular network of squares that you can number.

But the network itself has never really been there, see? And neither have the shapes—this collection of big stars looks like a dipper, and that array over there looks like a belt, and one way over there looks somewhat like a cross, and there's one over to the left that by some extreme wrangling can be made to look like a virgin. All these imaginary lines that seem to join the constellations together are our ways of projecting a pattern upon this great and glorious confusion so that we can remember it and chart it. But it's obvious that if you looked at these collections of stars from some completely different position in the galaxy, all of those constellations and arrangements would vanish. You'd have to invent new ones because there is nowhere static where the stars actually are. It all depends on where you're looking from.

This is how we figure out nature with our extraordinary symmetrical brains. It is we who introduce the law into the world. We invent it. The word *invent* in Latin means "to discover," but we don't discover something that's out there. When we invent the laws of nature, what we are discovering is something about ourselves, namely, our own passion for regularity, for prediction, and for keeping things under control.

Everything Is Context

Let's return to the billiards analogy. When you watch someone play the game of billiards, the cue hits the first ball, and that ball moves and hits another ball, which in turn moves and strikes another, and so on. You can observe that sequence and explain the behavior of the final ball that drops into the pocket in causal terms—the action is a chain of rational events that began with the strike of the cue.

This is precisely how most people today view the world—as something that occurs via the mechanical processes of cause and effect. They might admit that the larger picture is quite complicated, but would still argue that if one could know and track all the factors involved, you'd uncover that any behavior or singular act is the ineluctable result of a series of balls bouncing against each other and that fundamental atoms or atomic particles predisposed a particular event to occur just as it did. Technically, this is known as a *catenary* relationship. This is how we believe atoms work, in the same way as when we line up a row of dominoes or bricks, knock the first one down, and then watch as the others all fall down in turn. That's a catenary sequence.

However, it has become increasingly obvious to physicists and biologists that this will not do as a sufficient description of how various events affect each other.

There's a much different way of describing relationships. The word *reticulate* comes from the Latin word meaning "net" or "netlike." Applied to relationships, reticulation means that we cannot ascribe any given event to one or more previous events in a causal chain, but that the relationship between the past and the present—as well as between the present and the future—has to be taken into consideration before we can actually understand any given event.

Let's say I drop a ball and it bounces. Now, this might actually be considered multiple events, but for the sake of argument let's just call it one. I could say that I let the ball go, it obeyed a particular law of nature known as gravity, and it subsequently hit the floor. And because it was made of rubber and had some air inside, it bounced back up into the air and slightly disobeyed gravity for a moment or two.

But it's not enough just to describe the historical sequence of events that led to the ball bouncing, as if it were a series of causes and effects laid out on a string along a line of time. In actuality, everything depends upon a present context—the density of air, to begin with. All kinds of things must coexist in order for me to drop the ball in the first place, much less everything and everyone that goes into manufacturing such a toy. In this way, whatever happens must not be considered merely as a historical phenomenon; it must also be considered in context.

{ The whole notion of a thing or an isolated event in nature . . . is a purely abstract idea that does not fit the facts of nature at all. }

Most of us know that context is terribly important. It isn't just *when* a thing happens that's important; it's *where* it happens—that is, *in what setting*. The blood in my veins is in a certain setting, but in a test tube it's in a completely different setting. My blood does not behave in a test tube the same way it behaves while in my body. It isn't the same thing.

Similarly, we behave one way in a particular social setting and quite differently in another. When I was a child, I was one boy when I was at home with my parents, a different boy when I was with my aunt and uncle, and quite a different boy entirely when I was with my peers. I changed according to the setting I found myself in, as do most other children and adults.

In spite of this, we're told that we're supposed to be one consistent person, even though we're not. As we grow up, it's drummed into our heads that we should have a consistent character, just as a character in a novel is supposed to remain consistent throughout the narrative in order to come across as believable. Who behaves the same way all of the time? Doing so across various circumstances and in the company of various people doesn't mean you're consistent—it means you've become rigid and inflexible.

Everything depends on the context in which it is found. Anything we single out depends on its network relationship to everything else that's going on. In fact, the whole notion of a thing or an isolated event in nature—as well as the notion of causal relationships between different things and events—is a purely abstract idea that does not fit the facts of nature at all. In nature, there are no separate events. Nothing happens in isolation—not touching your head, not holding someone else's hand, not looking at the stars, not breathing—nothing.

Of course, you can see all sorts of wiggles happening around you—all sorts of colors and all sorts of shapes and forms—but none of them are actually separate things. We speak of inside and outside as distinct, but we can't truly separate them. Try doing that with your skin—it takes the outside and the inside working together to create this whole skin situation in the first place. No outside, no inside.

It's the same way with breathing. The physical situation of my body inhaling and exhaling is impossible without the external situation of there being air to breathe. You can't see air, but it's always around, so you don't pay much attention to it unless it changes rapidly, as in the case of a gale. And you can point out that change to someone else—that sudden wiggling going on out there—and say, "Hey, look at *that*." And they'll know what you mean by *that* because a *that* is something at the end of a finger point. That's different and peculiar from other things.

From that process comes the idea of an isolated event or a thing. It's a *that*. But all of these *thats* that are happening aren't disconnected—they go with each other. My inside goes with the outside, my breathing goes with the air, and this whole situation of you reading or listening to these words in this moment is a complicated *going-withness*.

Going With

This is the fundamental idea I'm speaking of here—the idea of *going with*. From this idea we can start to construct and understand the whole notion of networks, the principles of which are difficult to understand, especially for those of us brought up speaking Western languages and thinking in Western terms. That being said, it's possible for us to think of networks through the lenses of relativity and relationship.

Let's say you're sitting there being exactly the sort of person you are—maybe a little neurotic, maybe a little happy, maybe a little sick physically, maybe a little ashamed of yourself for one reason or the other . . . You're simply sitting there being however you're being, just the way you are. Whatever that's like for you—whatever your personal situation is—that experience goes with the entire situation of the rest of the universe. Back goes with front, inside goes with outside, and whatever you are goes with the way the whole of the rest of boundless being is arranged.

Now, you might think that it's the way that the boundless being is arranged that determines what you are, or conversely you might believe that you are what determines the structure or pattern of the larger universe—either you did it or it did you. I'll discuss that in more detail later.

For now, I'll just say that the argument of that dichotomy is ridiculous—it isn't a question of what controls what. It all goes together. You and the universe are one event. As Pierre Teilhard de Chardin famously writes in *The Phenomenon of Man*, the whole universe is the only true atom.[1] In other words, the universe is the only truly indivisible whole.

It's particularly hard for Westerners to grasp this idea. One reason it's difficult for us to understand that everything we are goes with the rest of the universe is that we're given conflicting messages about who we are. On one hand, we're supposed to be one consistent person; on the other, we're also supposed to improve and change. For one reason or the other, we're supposed to be different or better than we actually are.

We repeat this message to one another, we get the same idea from television, and we're bombarded with all sorts of advertisements saying the same thing. The world is full nowadays of people making a living from their systems—systems that show us how to grow, to evolve, to change in a particular direction. All for a fee, of course. They all say some version of "Look here—I've got this important program or school, and you really should come and study with me." The system might not originally be theirs—it might actually belong to some famous sage or pundit or other sort of spiritual authority they know—but it doesn't matter in the end. What matters is that you realize that you're supposed to change, which means you enact a particular course of study, which means that you pay.

I've been given all kinds of opinions about what I'm supposed to do with my life—for example, what I need to do in order to get myself into shape. A half hour of yoga practice, an hour of zazen, exercises to help my memory, a special diet to make sure I get proper nutrition, and so on. If I followed all of the advice I received, I'd spend my entire day doing things in the name of getting prepared for life. And when I think it through, I think, *My God . . . the whole damn project just isn't worth it.*

We receive subtle versions of these messages, of course. Some experts will tell you to just pick one thing. "You're getting confused," they say. "Narrow it down and focus on one thing." And if you're not sure which one thing to choose, they'll be sure to inform you about which one they think is best and right for you. This is precisely how people get drawn in and sewn up by religious fanatics—they get shown the proper way, whatever that is supposed to be.

I want to be clear that I'm not offering anything of the sort. I have no intention of selling you a system or program. I don't have any magic recipe that involves, say, something special for you to do every morning for five minutes or so. My whole intention here is to help set you free from all of that. Ideally, you only attend one seminar or read just one book and never have to come back to me again. It's not the best business model, but as far as my livelihood is concerned, there are always more people out there foolish enough to pay attention to me.

It shouldn't be about me anyway; it's about you. And you are like a dewdrop suspended on a multidimensional spider's web in the light of early morning. But if you look at that dewdrop closely, you'll see that it reflects every other dewdrop there is. And the way that one drop looks goes with the way that all the others appear, see? They each have their particular glimmer, depending on their peculiar position in the cosmos, and the reflection of the whole web in each drop of dew is slightly different. Nevertheless, the whole network—that is, all of the drops together—depends on each individual dewdrop, just as each individual dewdrop depends on all of the others.

So that's the situation we're living in. That mutuality can affront our logic at first, because although we might understand how we depend on the universe—after all, we need sunlight and air and water and parents and all that kind of thing—it's a lot more difficult to see how the universe depends on us. We've failed to learn that the relationship of the network is entirely mutual—it runs both ways. It depends on you just as much as you depend on it.

It's your brain that turns vibrations of air into sound. It's you that turns whatever the sun does into light. It's you that makes the air's activity in the sky into the color called blue. Blue doesn't exist on its own—there's only blue in your brain. If you hit a drum and the drum doesn't have any skin, it won't make any sound. It's the skin that evokes the noise out of a moving hand or drumstick. No skin, no noise.

Just as the dewdrop reflects everything else on the web, you reflect everything that goes on in the universe. By the constitution of what kind of reflector you are, you evoke what we call *sun*, *moon*, and *stars*. *Nebulas*, even.

Space itself is only vast in relation to you. Vastness means nothing on its own—it requires your participation and perception. From other perspectives, the space between stars could be minuscule, or the space between two hairs on your arm could be incredibly vast.

Again, the core principle I want to get across here is the idea of going with. The universe around you is your outside just as much as the organs inside your skin are your inside. You go with the universe in the same way that the stalk goes with the root, or the pistil with the stamen, or the North Pole with the South. The principle of relationship governs everything. Actually, I shouldn't say *governs*. Sometimes we have to use wretched terms just to approximate what we mean. Perhaps *underlies* is a better choice. Relationship underlies everything.

I want to repeat that the larger universe doesn't control or determine the smaller individual any more than the smaller individual actuates the larger universe. It's not a question of control; it's a question of dancing. It's a question of *what happens* rather than *what makes it happen*. Things aren't made to happen. You can only think that way if you insist that a certain event is quite separate, and then you can argue that the sequence of events that came before it made it happen in such and such a way. But in doing so you'd have to ignore the importance of context.

If you realize that everything is part of one event—that everything is a different aspect or phase of the same event—then you understand that it is simply happening. You don't see anything make it happen. As the Taoists say, everything is interrelated, and therefore we can observe patterns in the activity of the whole. There's an order to it—the order of the net.

Each square or knot of the net is involved in maintaining the larger order. Each knitted stitch holds the whole thing together—if one starts to go, the whole thing begins to unravel. Buddhism teaches that everything mutually interpenetrates everything else, and even Christianity has the symbol of the Holy Trinity with three interlocking rings. Take one of those rings away and the symbol loses its meaning. A given planet or star seems to move and operate on its own, but its behavior only makes sense when you examine the larger situation of interdependence.

If there were only one star in the whole universe, no motion could be ascribed to it. It couldn't even be said to stand still. Nobody could tell what it was doing because there wouldn't be anything for it to relate to. But if there were two stars, we might observe them getting closer or farther away from each other, although we wouldn't be able to tell which of them was moving. We'd need three stars to make a judgment about that—two of them might be closer together than the other one, which would make it seem like it was moving away from the pair. But maybe the two were moving away in unison. It's either "Hey, we don't like you, we're getting out of here" or "Hey, why don't you like me, why do you keep moving away?" How would we be able to tell who's right? We'd need a fourth star as an umpire. Two stars can only move in a straight line with respect to each other; three stars can move in a plane with respect to each other; it takes another star to establish an objective dimension. But then there's a new argument—which of them is the fourth star?

> *{ Anything that is part of the functioning of the whole is legitimate. }*

So that's the basic principle on which the whole universe is constructed. Motion depends on comparison with something that remains relatively still. There can't be any motion without comparison.

In this way, every single individual implies everything else that's going on in the universe. With lasers, you can photograph a small fragment of any photographic negative and from that tiny fragment reconstruct the larger picture from which it was taken, because the crystalline tensions in that given fragment imply the whole context of crystalline tensions that belong to that particular negative. In exactly the same way, you as an individual imply the world, and the world mutually implies you. You are a natural formation. You are not determined by the universe—you move in and with it as harmoniously as waves upon the ocean, as leaves upon a tree, as clouds in the sky.

We don't accuse the clouds of making aesthetic mistakes. Seen in the same light, all human beings are perfect forms of nature. You may have fashionable discriminations about who is beautiful and who is ugly, you may have metaphysical discriminations about who is sick and who is healthy, and you may have moral discriminations about who is good and who is evil, but these are all points of view—relative points of view. Anything that is part of the functioning of the whole is legitimate. Therefore, even your relative points of view are legitimate, as they, too, are a part of nature.

The key is to live on multiple levels at once. If you can do that, you'll find there are no mistakes. Everything moves in accordance with the Tao—the way of nature. And if you're close to that basic feeling, you'll always be sane. At the same time, you can also choose to participate in a more restricted point of view, wherein things are either good or bad, just as in any given room we can say that there's an *up* direction as well as a *down*. But you'd also know that in any area, there is no actual up and down—the terms are merely relative.

These two points of view don't contradict one another. However, if you only take the discriminatory point of view—that is, that there's a fundamental difference between good and evil—you'll come away with the Christian hang-up. That basic difference leads to the construction of an eternal heaven and an eternal hell, and the distinction between the two couldn't be more radical. And the result of that belief is a disease called chronic guilt, which is one of the most destructive emotions that anybody could have. You end up feeling like an outcast from the universe, at odds with reality and God himself. This makes people quite mad, and it's responsible for a good deal of the craziness of Western civilization.

That's not to say that there isn't an important distinction between good and evil; it's just that the distinction isn't fundamentally important in the bigger picture. You have to learn to admit varying degrees of importance—you can't just say that because a certain distinction isn't absolute, it isn't important. After all, your own physical formation isn't absolute, but it's clearly important.

You have a psychophysical organism. At the same time, you are something that the whole cosmos is doing. For the most part, I consider modern astrology to be pseudoscience, but there's significant truth in the practice of drawing a map of a person's soul that correlates to a map of the universe. It might be a crude picture, but it's the design of that person's individuality.

Your soul is something that contains your body. Your body doesn't have your soul inside it like some kind of spook. The whole cosmos is your soul. The cosmos is doing you at the point you call here and now. Reciprocally, you are doing the universe—one depends upon the other. As Westerners, we have difficulty holding these differing ideas simultaneously because we have been brainwashed by several centuries of two contrasting put-down theories of our nature. On the one hand, we've been informed that we are wretched, disobedient little subjects of an eternal king. On the other, we're told that we're simply a fortuitous congress of atoms in a mindless mechanism of incredible vastness. Having entertained those two theories for so long, we are unable to see that we and the universe are mutually causative or—to use the Chinese expression—mutually arising.

What We Mean by Intelligence

There's a significant hurdle for the average Westerner whose common sense and view of the universe is derived from the philosophies and scientific thought prominent in the nineteenth century. On the one hand, the organization of the universe was said to be intelligent, reflecting the dominant theism that presented God anthropomorphically as an old gentleman in the sky with whiskers. On the other hand, we were informed that God was dead beyond recall.

What does this mean in terms of an intelligent universe? Let's begin with the word *intelligence*, which is difficult enough to describe. It's like the word *love*—it seems like we all know what it means, but just try to define it. It's the same thing with the terms *time* and *space*.

Now, there are certain elements of intelligence that most of us would agree to. We would probably include complexity as an element, with the understanding that complexity is an orderly arrangement of different clusters of intricacy. But that gets us into another bind—what do we mean by *orderly*? Are we indicating with that particular word that everything is in order, as if intelligently arranged?

We use a lot of words that are imprecise. We recognize them when they appear, but we're not quite sure what they mean, and we just let it go at that. What if we began with the pure hypothesis that we ourselves are intelligent? We might as well make that assumption because if we are not intelligent, then nothing is. So, continuing on, for the sake of argument we'll say that we human beings are actually intelligent. Now, if that is the case, then it follows that the environment in which we live must also be intelligent because we are symptoms of that environment. One goes with the other. You would have a most difficult time convincing me that intelligent symptoms are possible in an unintelligent organization.

We belong to this world. We didn't arrive here from somewhere else. We're not tourists in this universe—we are expressions of it, just as branches or fruit are expressions of trees. You won't find intelligent organisms living in unintelligent environments anywhere. The environment in which we live is a system of mutual cooperation among various organisms—a vast complexity of different kinds of organisms—and the total balance of all of that makes your life possible. Front to back, human life goes with an extremely complex bacteriological world that occasionally diseases us but for the most part assists us with its colonies, societies, and methods of reproduction. Our blood and veins and bones and intestines and all of that depend on that world, and that's just looking at the bacteriological level.

The world of insects is also tremendously important to us. If you speak with an educated entomologist, they will scare the wits out of you because they'll reveal a number of conclusive reasons why the insects will ultimately take over the world. In the meantime, we are not absolutely dominated by flies, because there are enough spiders to go around. And then there are the birds and flowers to consider. Birds and insects are mutually necessary to each other, as are flowers and insects, especially the bees. They might look quite different, but from one point of view you could say that flowers and bees are different aspects of the same organism because you can't have one without the other. Into this interdependent mix, throw in the complexities of atmospheric qualities and so on, and you quickly realize that what you call your body and brain are utterly involved in this network of other kinds of organisms.

You don't find chicken eggs without hens, nor do you see hens without eggs—a hen is, in one way, an egg's way of becoming more hens and eggs. It all goes together, but Westerners have trouble seeing this because we are primarily invested in using an analytical method of perception that spotlights particular features of the world. Furthermore, we only give names and symbols to the features of the world that we consider significant, and there are many features of the world that we outright ignore. Young children point and ask, "What is that?" But we can't answer them unless we recognize what they're noticing and consider it important. What's the word for dry space? What do we call the inside surface of a tube? Why do the Inuits have different names for snow, and Aztecs employed only one for snow, rain, hail, ice, and so on?

Naming those things we consider important means isolating those things as separate entities. But they are only separate in a purely theoretical way and just because we say so—they're not actually materially or physically separate. It is immensely important that we become aware of this fact because when we aren't aware of it we do the most stupid things. We try to solve problems by attacking the symptoms of those problems, as in the case of our attempts to abolish mosquitoes. We forget that mosquitoes go with a certain kind of environment, and when we kill all of the mosquitoes we change that environment—for example, we end up killing the other creatures that depend on mosquitoes for their existence.

For the same reason, before injecting the human organism with drugs or altering it with certain operations, you must study the body in great detail or risk bringing about unpredictable and unfavorable consequences. We must also thoroughly understand the ecology of an area before farming, and we can readily see that not doing so has appalling results. And in order to overcome our characteristic sense of hostility to the external world and stop conquering nature with bulldozers and space with rockets, we have to realize that the universe is just as much ourselves as our own bodies are. We have an inside body and an outside body, and the two are inseparable. This inseparability should give every technologist pause, because you probably shouldn't go running into a particular situation with penicillin and DDT and what have you because how do you know when to stop? Without knowing it, you could be discriminating against a surplus of a given aspect—say, crickets or stomach flora—and will subsequently have to build the population up again or risk the consequences.

This is why the Taoists teach *wu wei*. It means something like "noninterference," especially when it comes to nature and politics. It's almost like our concept of laissez-faire, but not quite, because the Taoists understand that acting upon nature is unavoidable—you can't actually isolate yourself from the world. You interfere with something with every breath you take. The art of wu wei is that when you do interfere, you endeavor to do so by going with the grain. If you want to split wood, split it with the grain. If someone attacks you, use judo; the other person's violence will bring about their downfall. Similarly, sailing is very wu wei, whereas rowing typically isn't.

Unlike what transpired in the West, the Taoists viewed the cosmos as a vast, universal organism without a boss. In Chinese philosophy, there isn't anyone out there making the world happen or ordering it to do so. There's no central principle in the middle and nothing that sends out commands to all of its subordinate parts. Instead, the thing intelligently organizes itself.

{ What would you change if you were God? }

This is the principle of *ziran*, which means "self so" or "what is so of itself." For Taoists, the whole universe is a self-so, self-regulating organism, and the individual is not merely a part of that larger organism but an expression of the whole thing. And, as I've mentioned elsewhere, the whole depends on this particular expression just as much as the expression depends upon the whole. The Japanese term *jijimuge* addresses this principle of mutual interpenetration as well.

But, you see, when we look at the larger whole, it remains a bit of a puzzle, and we come up with all sorts of objections to calling it *intelligent*. We can think of a number of improvements we'd like to make, as if by some conscious science we could just reconstruct the universe and remove the need for mosquitoes or reorganize the human body in a more optimal way. It goes without saying that adding our improvements would result in other consequences, and we likely wouldn't enjoy all of them. Hence the saying "Be careful what you wish for."

What would you change if you were God? What kind of universe would you design? Really think it through sometime. I strongly believe that if you went through the trouble of modeling your own universe and seeing what comes of it, you'd eventually settle on the exact model we have now. All of these fundamental principles—vibration, energy, and the yin-yang balance of negative and positive elements—make up this model, which is incredible.

Even so, we have difficulty seeing the universe as an intelligent organism. Physicists have made maps to describe the behavior of nuclei that include rotating particles or wavicles—they look more mathematical than a living organism because we expect an organism to look sort of gooey with flesh and blood and so on. If you just look through a microscope, you might not see the organism, but when you look out the other way at the rest of the universe, here we are, as if sitting down and moving around on one of those electrons. One of the reasons it's difficult for us to formulate the idea that there is an intelligence operating here is because all we're capable of seeing is a fireworks display—the big show of radioactive molten gas. So much escapes our conscious inspection, and we can't see the total design.

So we make the mistake of viewing the universe as a contraption of sorts and think of ourselves as something that just happened to arrive upon it by accident. It's funny that we can put ourselves down by saying we're just an accident, a kind of chemical accident that has occurred on an unimportant rock that orbits a lesser star on the fringe of a minor galaxy. And that's supposed to be us, floating around in a universe that doesn't give a damn about us. At the same time, this wretched little chemical accident is capable of reflecting an image of the whole vast cosmos inside its tiny head—and is aware that it is doing so. So we are small in dimension but vast in comprehension. Which one of those aspects is more important?

If we are capable of seeing—that is, from a strictly scientific point of view—that an individual organism goes with its environment (bees with flowers, flowers with grubs, grubs with birds, and so on), then how can we define ourselves as merely that which occurs inside our skin? Everything that goes on within our body goes with everything happening outside of it, thereby constituting a single complex field of diversified behaviors and processes. Even when you look at it just from a physical point of view, the network becomes obvious.

But reading books on ecology and botany and zoology and astronomy and physics and so on will only result in a type of theoretical realization of what I'm talking about.

By itself, that type of realization won't take us very far. Specifically, it won't have all that much effect on how we live from day to day. That level of change requires a knowledge of a more emotionally compelling nature. If we want to change the way we act with respect to our environment—for example, to prevent ourselves from continuing to destroy it as we are currently doing—then we need a lot more than just theoretical knowledge.

Ecological Awareness

The United States Congress has passed legislation to make burning the American flag a serious offense. This was accompanied by lots of patriotic speeches and rhetoric and much reciting of poems. It's the most fantastic example of American confusion between symbol and reality that you could think of because the same Congress is directly or indirectly responsible for burning up what the flag actually stands for, which is the geographical United States and its people. Legislation like this is passed at the same time that nothing substantive is done as forests are being devastated, the water and atmosphere are being polluted, natural resources are becoming depleted, and a type of economy is being propagated that under sane circumstances would be termed sheer lunacy. We cannot distinguish between symbols and reality because we've all been hypnotized with words and symbols, which is one primary reason why theoretical knowledge will only take us so far.

When a flag is more precious than its actual country, one can definitively say that insanity is in play. When people mistake saluting a flag for loving their country, they are sadly mistaken. Loving one's country means participating in its life in a loving and considerate way, not killing off its creatures with poisonous insecticides and so on. We fail to see that the outside world is not a kind of chunk of mineral resource that we can exploit at will. For us to consume beef, someone must farm cattle—it requires people to conduct husbandry and take care of the cows. It's the same thing with fishing. And because we have not properly husbanded whales, they're becoming extinct. This is the price we pay. If you live off animals, as most of us do, it would be wise to cherish them.

I will add to this a particular prejudice of mine. One of the main ways we can cherish the animals we eat is to cook them properly. When our primary aim is to simply chew and ingest what's supposed to give us energy and nourishment, it reveals an irreverent relationship with those now-dead animals and plants. Their lives deserve our reverence; it's simply the proper response. Accordingly, the act of cooking should be similar to the rituals of a priest at an altar, and kitchens should not be looked upon simply as laboratories in which we throw things together for consumption at the other end.

But all of this requires, you see, a situation in which human beings are vividly aware of the external world as something as much themselves as are their own bodies. What we see *out there* is not merely something external—it's in our head, and our head's in it. They mutually interpenetrate each other. And respect for the external world requires seeing it in much the same way as you view what's inside your skin. Most people look at a piece of wood as just a chunk of stuff, but that's not how a carpenter thinks—at least, not a very good one.

If we treat the things that seem to us *out there* as unfeeling, inert blocks of stuff, we're in for more trouble. We blow up mountains with dynamite because we don't consider mountains to be living beings. I was just visiting a group of Native Americans who told me that the continent of the United States will one day shake all of us off it, just as a dog shakes off fleas. The storms are going to get much worse. The earthquakes and floods and fires will also get worse. The pests are going to multiply in all sorts of strange ways until the continent eventually gets rid of us and leaves the land to the people who originally lived here and who still know how to treat it with reverence and respect.

When I talk in academic and scientific circles about these things, especially when they pertain to a mystical experience, I have to be careful about the terminology I use. I don't say *mystical experience*, actually; instead, I call it *ecological awareness*. That's a much more acceptable term in scholarly environments, and it really amounts to the same thing. The academy doesn't like to discuss mysticism, you see; for academics, it's a dirty word associated with intangible mist and vagueness.

To date, ecology has not quite come of age as a science. Well, perhaps it's more accurate to say that the importance of ecology, as a multidisciplinary science that studies the relationships between organisms and their environments, is widely recognized, but its existence on campuses today frequently runs afoul of departmental politics. Most universities are based on the long-standing idea that there are distinct departments of knowledge, although the classification and relative importance of these departments has always changed over time. For example, during the Middle Ages, the highest-ranking department was theology, which was considered then to be the queen of sciences, in much the same way that physics or chemistry is viewed today. Nowadays, theology has lost its high rank—there might be a department of religious studies, but it occupies an obscure set of rooms somewhere in the philosophy building, which itself is placed way off at the edge of campus.

Academic departments have never remained fixed entities for very long. The parent departments of biology and physics gave birth to biophysics; biology and chemistry begat the science of biochemistry; and from physics and astronomy we received astrophysics. And as the formations keep changing, there are difficult political consequences that arise for the simple reason that faculty members and the chairs of given departments are jealous of their positions. This is why when hybrid departments start out, the establishment always labels their adherents as dabblers. This is precisely how it is with scientists in the growing field of ecology, who are told ad nauseum that they should have a more thorough grounding in biology, zoology, botany, bacteriology, and so on.

For several reasons, this charge is absurd. In the academic world, students are typically required to complete various prerequisites; that is, they're made to take a certain course before they can take the next in the approved series. As it turns out, this approach is mostly unnecessary. As time goes on, students develop the ability to absorb bodies of knowledge without having the prerequisites, just as Einstein's theory of relativity is much easier to understand nowadays than it was in the distant past. You don't need an elaborate demonstration on a blackboard with all sorts of strange diagrams anymore—young people get it a lot more quickly. They have no more difficulty absorbing the basic principles of relativity than we once did absorbing the revolutionary notion that the earth is spherical as opposed to flat. Common sense changes over time, and a feeling for knowledge adjusts itself.

It's become obvious that there have to be ways of linking together the established departments of knowledge—physics, chemistry, history, anthropology, et cetera—which have been serving for the longest time as huge paving stones. It's always between the paving stones that the little things begin to grow, and the growing edge nowadays is in the interstices between these finite departments. Ecology is one of the most important interstices I can think of, especially in the modern world, because we're now equipped with a degree of technology never seen before in history, and we're applying the power of that technology to alter our environment. We should make sure we are doing so in a way that doesn't destroy it any further.

In the Chinese and Japanese view of nature, you don't find such a sense of hostility between the human organism and its environment but rather a sense of being one with it, with an accompanying emphasis on collaboration with nature. We don't have such a nuanced view in the West. Instead, one school of thought seems to want to push technological progress as far and as quickly as possible, and we can see the results of that approach everywhere—for example, it's how we get what I call *Los Angelization*: the proliferation of built communities that when you look at them appear more like clusters of cancer cells than anything of a biologically healthy nature. On the other hand, another approach in the West—one popular among young people who are digging the dropout scene—wants to get rid of all of the concrete, pretend to be Native Americans, and return to nothing but the green grass. These are two completely extreme points of view.

I'd like to explore the possibility of a middle way, one that views technology not as a purely unnatural manifestation but as a perfectly proper development of human capacities. At the same time, technology has to be used in the right spirit, with the right care, and in such a way that we do not irremediably disturb the balances of nature. In the balances of nature, no one species should get so out of hand as to become the top species and dominate all the others as human beings are trying to do.

The *I Ching*, also known as the *Book of Changes*, is an ancient text fundamental to Chinese ways of thinking. It's based on an analysis of the processes of nature in terms of the relative balancing of the two forces of yang and yin. Perhaps *forces* is not quite the right word because Taoists—and Buddhist and Hindus, for that matter—see the universe instead as a single system of energy. Even *energy* isn't the best choice because the word indicates something in motion, and we can't be aware of motion except in relation to stillness, and vice versa. Whatever this *energy-stillness* fundamentally is cannot be thought about, defined, or discussed in any way, and yet it is basic to everything we experience and do not experience.

This basic energy-stillness is like the diaphragm in a loudspeaker that bears all the sounds you hear on the radio—the human voice, all kinds of musical instruments, airplanes, automobiles, and so on—and the diaphragm makes no distinction whatsoever about what sound plays upon it. Everything you hear is actually a series of vibrations of that diaphragm, but the announcer doesn't come on first thing in the morning to announce that fact. Whenever any circumstance is constant, we tend in the course of time to ignore it, and so it is with that diaphragm. We don't think of it, but it is entirely essential. Without it, we couldn't hear anything whatsoever on the radio.

> { It is possible to realize that we
> are identical with the fundamental
> energy of the universe. }

Similarly, we don't typically talk about the substratum of the ground of being. From a logical point of view, it's absolutely meaningless to talk about anything that is common to everything. But the logical point of view does not embrace all forms of knowledge, and it is possible for us as human beings to become aware of this substratum—not as an object, not as something you can take out and look at, but nevertheless as something we can become strongly and sensuously aware of. Doing so, we can regain a new sense of our own identity, our own being—not as one of many things and not as one little event among many events that come and go, but a sense of one's actual self as *being*—the single energy field that can't be defined or identified.

By realizing that, perhaps we can remove the frantic anxiety of trying to endlessly secure ourselves as separate organisms, fighting other creatures and playing these elaborate games in our attempts to one-up each other. If we could do that, we could overcome the anxiety that leads us to regard nature itself as our enemy—an enemy that must be conquered and subjugated.

This realization is not the same thing as a belief or idea. The fundamental energy of the universe cannot be embraced in an idea, in a concept, in any collection of words, or in an explanation. It eludes all classification. You can't possess or catch hold of it. You are it, and if you try to possess it, you're implying that you aren't. In Zen, this is called "putting legs on a snake." Even so, people either try to catch hold of it or try to achieve it instead by doing nothing at all, but both of these approaches are actually attempts to capture it when there is absolutely no need to do so in the first place.

It is possible to realize that we are identical with the fundamental energy of the universe. It is our real self, and although it doesn't make a difference, all differences are in a way made by it, and therefore it makes the difference of differences. Nevertheless, it's completely basic.

It's as if we're a gambler who is extremely wealthy, but the game we're playing is actually for peanuts. Even so, we get absorbed in the game and become anxious about winning, and we feel angry or frustrated when we don't win. Are we going to lose all of our peanuts? In actuality, there's nothing to worry about, because peanuts are just peanuts. It's just that we become so absorbed in the game that we forget the larger context within which the game is happening.

In exactly the same way, every individual has become so myopically absorbed with the details of their birth and death that they have completely forgotten the context in which birth and death occur. We have been systematically and progressively hypnotized by our whole upbringing to believe that we are only this particular ego in this particular body, and we are so convinced of that belief that the context in which all of this happens is completely repressed.

Of Gods and Puppets

An organism and its environment are a single system of energy expressed with great complexity as one process, one activity. It's possible to become aware of this, not simply theoretically but as a matter of sensation. However, the feeling is at first curious and often misinterpreted. Some people experience the sensation of floating—that is, passively, not doing much of anything, not making any exertion of will—and it can seem like their behavior is simply happening. On the other hand, it can feel as if you are making everything happen, that you are controlling your environment in a godlike way. These are polar opposite ways of experiencing the same thing.

People sometimes experience this kind of sensation by accident and frequently jump to strange conclusions. It depends on their background, specifically their religious upbringing, because that's what gives them a language to understand the experience and express to themselves and to others how they feel. And it's important to understand this theoretically just in case it ever happens to you and people accuse you of being crazy.

The two interpretations of the experience I just presented—either that of being a sort of puppet or knocked-around billiard ball or that of being an independent source of energy responsible for pushing the world around—are both based on the same false assumption, which is that the individual organism is separate from the world. The background for the first interpretation involves Newton and Descartes, who both molded the common sense of the average person living today, even though science today—especially in physics and biology—has gone far beyond those limited points of view. Psychology is another matter, because Freud has been incredibly influential, and he conceived of the human psyche as analogous with hydraulics, which is a form of Newtonian mechanics. The unconscious is like deep water, for example, and sexual energy resembles the flow of a river—it can be dammed up, be repressed, move through channels and outlets, and so on. So Freudianism is a form of psychohydraulics.

The puppet type of experience—that is, the sensation of automatically responding to all of the physical and social influences around us—might feel objectionable or enjoyable. You might experience the sensation similar to a pleasant sort of floating, in which you don't have to do much of anything at all—with no problems to think about and no worries about what you ought to be doing. You simply feel yourself responding to different stimuli, and that could either feel quite pleasant or terribly threatening, depending on your personal constitution.

Have you ever felt that you were dreaming during the course of everyday life? That a particular experience wasn't quite real? This is a spooky feeling for some people. Occasionally, your mind slips off in a different direction, much like turning the dials on a radio—your mind wanders off and lands on a different station, and this station allows you to slip into another way of seeing things. This is the place where people experience accidental illuminations and psychotic episodes and all sorts of funny things like that, and in the context of what I'm talking about, you might interpret the experience as if you were on the end of a collection of strings manipulated by other events or intelligences, just like a puppet.

As I mentioned before, we have been conditioned to believe that part of our life is under our control and part of it is not. Again, this is the distinction between that which is voluntary (what we do) and that which is involuntary (that which we must passively accept). However, the borderline between those two is often unclear—let's take a look at breathing again as an example. Breathing is something we have to go on doing if we enjoy living, and we can easily acquire the sensation that we are consciously doing the breathing and controlling it according to our will, but breathing doesn't actually require our thinking about it, which is fortunate. In this case, the distinction between voluntary and involuntary is quite vague.

In a similar way, it can sometimes feel like we make decisions out of the blue—just like that, as if we didn't have any awareness leading up to the choice. It just seems that such a decision comes out of nowhere because our awareness of a lot of information has been screened out. Most of us interpret the act of making a decision as a different kind of act than growing our own hair, but in actuality the two aren't so different—we only think they are due to unawareness. But if our awareness were to change and we realized that everything happens—as the Chinese say—*of itself*, our backgrounds might lead us to believe that everything happens involuntarily and that we are actually left out of the decision-making like a puppet who must simply obey. But this, too, would be incorrect.

In truth, we don't have a system of nature that is either deterministic or voluntaristic. The individual is not a puppet who responds to their environment passively, but neither is the individual the center of all activity who controls and changes the environment at will. Both of these views are based on a lack of awareness. Instead, the behavior of the individual and the behavior of the environment are the same process. Now, you can look at this process from these two distinct points of view—that either it's all happening to you or you are somehow doing it all—but these are just two ways of looking at the same thing.

If you think that your nervous system is creating the external world somehow—that is to say that things such as light, weight, heat, color, and shape only exist in terms of human neurology—then it isn't a stretch to believe that your nervous system is what evokes the whole universe. But you can take the opposite point of view and believe that the human nervous system is something that exists in the external world and is entirely dependent on sunlight, air, the proper temperature, and so on. Both of these points of view are true, but as Westerners we aren't provided with a logic that empowers us to integrate them, which is why some people feel as if they are just floating around, passively responding to the operations of nature, and others believe they are an all-powerful God.

In truth, there is just one process. You can look at this process from different directions, but you can't really split it up. We are not merely acting upon the world, and we are not simply responding to its actions upon us, and the more we become familiar with this unfolding process, the more intelligent we become and act. Intelligence is a function of the degree to which we realize that our behavior is one with the behavior of the rest of the world.

{ The sound of the rain needs no translation. }

As I noted before, Teilhard says that the universe is the only true atom because it is not actually divisible. But this is left out of our ordinary awareness, because in our ordinary awareness we overlook the connections between so-called things and so-called events, making them little more than aspects of one event. It's as if we're looking at everything through a venetian blind so that particular intervals are ignored or cut out. We know that our senses are screening devices. The eye responds only to a narrow spectrum of the various forms of light vibrations—we don't see X-rays or cosmic rays, for example. The human ear, as well, responds only to a rather narrow spectrum of sound. And it isn't just that we screen out with our senses but with our thinking systems as well.

As a result, there are gaps in our awareness. For example, we tend to ignore space. We think that the space between us and the objects or people in our environment is basically nothing at all, that it isn't all that important. In fact, it's tremendously important. It's the space—the intervals—between tones in music, for example, that allows us to hear melody. Just like the diaphragm in the radio speaker that makes sound possible, space is that in which everything happens. Without space; no happening. That's how fundamentally important it is, and yet we ignore it.

We have been trained to regard only certain things as important. That's why meditation—at least as it's understood by Buddhists and Taoists—is so revealing because it helps you stop valuing and putting a price on all the various things you could be aware of. When you stop thinking about it and are simply aware, it suddenly strikes you that everything is equally important, and that allows you to feel amazed at things you never were amazed at before—absolutely fascinated. You hear the sound of rain outside, and it sounds just as important as the most profound thing anyone has ever said, and as a Zen teacher once told me, the sound of the rain needs no translation.

The distinctions we make between one thing and another are all conceptual. Cut the concepts and see them fresh, and there are no divisions—it's all one process. That's not to say that in the continuum of the physical world there are no lines, solids, spaces, and that kind of thing; it doesn't mean that if you saw the world correctly it would appear as a homogenized mass. It most likely appears precisely as it does now but at the same time as one continuous wiggle. It is, after all, a wiggly world. Look out of the window of an airplane as you fly sometime—look at how wiggly all of those clouds and mountains and hills are. Of course, then you'll see these squares and rectangles, but that's just human beings keeping themselves busy trying to straighten things out.

People disapprove of wiggles because wiggles are difficult to control. They're slippery. Also, you can't exactly count them very well. How do you count the wiggles in a cloud? And what constitutes a wiggle in the first place? If a wiggle comes with bumps, is each bump a subordinate wiggle? Once you start looking into it, especially when you look through a magnifying glass, wiggledom just goes on forever. So wiggles of the world, unite! You've got nothing to lose but your names.

Putting a name on a cloud doesn't do anything to it—it doesn't separate the cloud from the sky. Names are just socially agreed-upon divisions we use to describe the various forms of nature, but nature itself is formless in the sense that it is all one form, one process. We only break apart the great continuous wiggliness into things and events for the purposes of control, and yet all of our categorizing leaves the world undivided. It's simply a way of being able to talk about phenomena in order to agree how we are going to control them and decide what we're going to do with them.

Conventionally, when you say that there really are no things and no events, most people will become shocked or startled. It's an affront to common sense. This thing on my foot is a shoe, dammit—it's a thing, right here for us all to see. Except that it isn't a shoe at all.

The idea of separate things is an abstraction. As an organism, you are not something separate from your environment. A living organism is something like a flame—a flame might appear to be a thing that sits on top of a candle, but in actuality it is a stream of gas that is never the same from one microsecond to the next. It is a constant flow of energy. In the same way, our bodies appear to have a constant form, but we are a flowing of energy that keeps coming in and keeps going out.

Additionally, everything that could be recognized as a wiggle or unit of any kind exists only in relation to other phenomena. This, again, is the principle of mutual interpenetration. Anything that can be designated as part of something implies the whole, just as the whole implies the part. For this reason, clever archaeologists can reconstruct an entire creature from a single bone, because a particular jawbone implies a certain kind of skull and so on. And so every single thing in this world exists only in relation to the whole system. Existence is relationship. Yang cannot exist without yin, and it's their relationship that enables them both—solid and space, up and down, life and death, being and nonbeing.

If I shout in a nonresonating environment, there won't be a noise. You can't make waves in a vacuum. In just the same way, existence is relationship. Society constitutes every one of us, and we are who we are as individuals because of this interlocking complex of human communities. We are who we are as people because of our roles in relationship to groups of other people, specifically those with which we move, just as we learned to change our behavior when we were children depending on the company we found ourselves in. Personally, I have a hard time with the notion of fixed social roles. This probably explains why I enjoy playing tricks.

As I've said elsewhere, how we are depends on the context in which we find ourselves, just as the meaning of a given word depends on the sentence or paragraph in which it is placed. We already have great skill at breaking things down into their component parts, but by only applying the analytical mind in that way, we neglect the other side of things that takes into account the context of each individual wiggle. It's important to define wiggles, but you can't really do so unless those wiggles have an environment. The outside of the wiggle is just as important as the inside, and it's the outside that we habitually overlook.

When a snake moves, it curls. One side of the snake becomes convex, whereas the other is concave. Which side moves first? They both move together. And so it is with our inside world and outside world, which are not different. They are different in the sense that one is inside and the other is outside, but they are not different in the sense that they are not separate, and so they move together. It's just that we're unaware of it, mostly due to a kind of psychological myopia of being hung up on a particular way of looking at things.

Klesha is a Buddhist term in Sanskrit that we normally translate as "attachment" or "defiling passion." However, a better translation into modern American English would be something like "hang-up." We get hung up on a fixed way of thinking—in this case, that the world is divided up in such and such a way—and so we fail to see the going-withness of it all. We don't see that insides are inseparable from their outsides and that organisms go with their particular environments, and so we consider our body as something other than unified. From one point of view, we're just an accumulated mass of cells. Take physics into account, and you're not even that—you're just molecules, atoms, subatomic particles, wavicles, and the vast spaces in between wavicles. But what is it that ties all that stuff together?

When the leaves start to come back on the trees in spring, you could look at them as new leaves. Last year's leaves fell off the tree in the autumn, and now a new generation of leaves has arisen to take their place. But if you look at it from another point of view, you'd just say that the tree is leafing again—leafing is just something that the tree does from time to time. It's only because we're so fascinated with the individual details of people that we think that there are generations upon generations of different humans on the planet, but a being from Mars observing the continual process of our birth and death might just as easily think that it's the same thing happening to our planet repeatedly—humans keep on coming, but it's actually the same ones who keep coming back. In the same way, every year's leaves are the same old leaves coming back. They die, they're reabsorbed, and they keep coming back on the tree.

Everything does this. Everything keeps doing it again, but there are these spaces in between, coming and going, and when we just look at those spaces, we don't see anything, so we think that the wave is finished—it's done. And we think that when we die, our life is finished, and that's too bad. But what we really are is the energy field itself, and that energy field keeps doing us. It keeps peopling. And it's you who keeps peopling. Who else would be responsible?

Of course, we can't admit that we're responsible for all of this. The whole game is to pretend that we aren't.

2

Civilizing
Technology

The great civilizations of the East—particularly the Chinese and Japanese—did not develop the same sort of technology as did Europe and the United States. Accordingly, they faced different problems than we did, and for that we labeled them backward. They had different issues with disease and famine and poverty, so we didn't think that we could learn anything from them—their forms of civilization hadn't accomplished the things that we'd done. We ignored the fact that our own technology and particular progress has been fairly recent, that until the middle of the nineteenth century it was perfectly ordinary to live with torture, slavery, child labor, filth of unspeakable proportions, plagues, and all of that sort of thing. That's just the way it was, but we've forgotten it. We have short memories.

There's a church hymn I remember from childhood that goes something like

> All things bright and beautiful,
> All creatures great and small,
> All things wise and wonderful,
> The Lord God made them all.
>
> . . . .
>
> The rich man in his castle,
> The poor man at his gate,
> God made them high and lowly
> And ordered their estate.[1]

I would guess that last verse has since been eliminated from the hymn because it says that all stations in life—fortune and misfortune, riches and poverty—are determined and ordered by God. It says that nothing can be done about it, and people tend to accept states of affairs about which nothing can be done. And nothing much could be done about one's station in life, really, until the Industrial Revolution came along, at which point everybody wanted to do quite a bit about it, which is where technology came into play.

So the technologies that developed around the world varied for all sorts of reasons, including reasons that are entirely geographical. When you look at a map of Europe, you'll notice that it's quite wiggly—it's full of inlets, islands, harbors, coves, and all that sort of thing. By contrast, China and India are solid land masses, which in part explains why, by comparison, Europeans became preeminently sailors.

And it's highly possible that our first great technological discoveries were the work of seafaring people who had their own particular culture, who knew that the world was round, and who became peerless navigators. Their first true houses may even have been overturned boats. The cross-fertilization of different civilizations and cultures really took off due to sea travel, and the machinery and innovation involved in that exchange required substantial innovation. Sailing is a direct exemplification of people and nature in cooperation.

As far as technology goes, rowing is quite different. It's a rather unintelligent way of propelling a boat because it requires a great deal of effort. Sailing, on the other hand, simply uses the energy of nature to move the boat—you flow through nature effortlessly by using the forces around you in a clever way, which is the wu wei principle in Taoism. I mentioned before that wu wei means something like "noninterference," but it is also sometimes incorrectly translated as "non-action." Wu wei is acting, but in accordance with the field of forces in which you find yourself. Therefore, a skillful person will inquire into the nature of those forces, and a Taoist would ask, "What is its *li*?"—the word *li* meaning the organic pattern of the situation.

When you know the pattern of a given situation, you can act in accordance with it and not overly force things. If you are sawing wood and push the saw too hard, the cut will become jagged—people who saw impatiently always make a mess of it. Of course, you must use your muscles when sawing, but if you see that the saw is sharp enough and work with its weight, you'll have the sensation that the saw is doing most of the work, and if you do that, then you will make a good cut. You'll find this in other crafts as well. When you sing well, it feels as if the song is singing itself; when you drive well, the car and the road just carry you along in a skillful way. When you do anything skillfully, you're expressing the total power of the field of forces, which is expressing itself in the form of skillful action through the agency of you as a human organism. It requires intelligence to do this.

The Problem of Abstractions

There's another internal reason why the Chinese developed technology in the way that they did. In stark contrast to Taoism, Confucianism is not all that interested in nature. Confucian thought focuses on human relations and is very scholastic, and the great classics of Confucianism had an ordering but rigidifying effect on Chinese culture. It's like that with anything that views the written word as an ultimate authority—Christianity, Islam, science, health, and so on. The theologians of Galileo's day wouldn't look through his telescope because their good book had already explained how the universe worked, and that book just couldn't be wrong. The same thing still goes on today in science. Whenever somebody advances a new scientific position that the mainstream considers outrageous, scientists will dismiss it outright—"That's impossible! It couldn't be!"—and that's because they are rigidly defending a conception of the universe that requires everything to be as dull as possible.

We're given an interpretation of the universe that is boring and stupid. Anything that looks into or reveals something that science can't account for is simply ignored. Science only studies the usual. In order to study an event scientifically, it must happen several times. Sometimes when you get sick and go to the doctor, your symptoms change or vanish, just like when that funny noise your car was making earlier disappears the moment you present it to the mechanic. It's like that with scientists, too. Whenever they do try to study something unusual, it typically doesn't occur again, and so they say that it never happened.

Just as the Confucians got too hung up on books, we have become too hung up on our abstract concept of nature, so much so that we cannot experience things outside the framework of our limited conceptual understanding. But when a conceptual system no longer takes into account the constantly changing pattern of reality, it no longer serves us. In fact, it can get us into trouble.

The Taoists had a different conceptual system, and it was quite interested in nature. Taoist texts are full of natural illustrations, and the behaviors of water, insects, and the elements are all used as illustrations of the art of life. The Confucians, on the other hand, were lexicographers—they believed in the reification of names and strove to create clear and rigid definitions of words so that people would use them in the right way. But then the Taoists asked them,

"With what words will you define the words? And with what words will you define the words you use to define those other words?" The situation is obviously circular, and dictionaries themselves are entirely circular. To someone who doesn't know the given language at all, a dictionary without illustrations and pictures is an impenetrable, closed system. This is why the Taoists laughed at the Confucians, because their view of nature was not abstract, rigid, and codified but organic and flowing—a single, living organism of immense complexity. They didn't see the universe as consisting of separate parts. The head goes with the feet, the stomach goes with the brain, and everything arises mutually together. Aspects might be said to be different from one another, but that doesn't mean that they're separate.

For this reason, the Taoists are very cautious about interfering with anything, especially when it comes to politics. Confucian politics are based on ideas of rulership—a strict, top-down hierarchical structure of authority that must be obeyed by those below. But the Taoist advice to rulers in the *Tao Te Ching* stresses humility, following the Tao, exercising restraint, building relationships with citizens, and so on. The text also says that the Tao loves and nourishes all things and people without lording it over them. For Taoists, the ideal emperor was more like a sanitation engineer than a mayor—retiring and inconspicuous. The emperor was supposed to have a kind of anonymous quality, because the Taoists felt that you most foster cooperation when you let people cooperate rather than compelling them to do so.

We don't see the world as a living organism in the West, which is also revealed in our technological advancements. Instead, we view the world as a mechanism, and for us a mechanism is an assemblage of replaceable parts that has a particular governor. An organism, on the other hand, might have several important governors that work together in a reticulate pattern, much as the brain and stomach do in the human body. Now, which one of those organs is more important? Some people will say the stomach is because eating is the most important thing, but the brain is what enables the stomach to find food. That's actually why it evolved—to better help the eyes and ears sneak around and discover things to swallow. And some people will say that the stomach is merely a forerunner for the most important character to arrive on the scene and that all the stomach does is provide fuel to the brain to do whatever it does.

Both of these theories are partially correct. The actual arrangement between stomach and brain is mutual, and the two arise and work together. In a mechanical, hierarchical, boss-based system, it's different. When you have a machine, and an operator and an engineer who put it all together, you have a government—a monarchical world order. And then we use further mechanical techniques to make people behave differently, even going so far as developing a special technological device to chop off their heads.

We Need a New Analogy

Another reason we developed the technology we did in the West is because Newtonian mechanics arises out of the theory that the physical world is an artifact created by a super cosmic engineer who governs everything from above by law. Out of this comes the belief that things behave according to mechanical causality, and this leads to forms of technology that look like steam engines, automobiles, hydraulic systems, electricity, and everything like that.

The mechanical analogy served us well up to a point. But we've long since reached a stage of development and made profound discoveries in quantum physics and biology that suggest that a more organic way of viewing everything is clearer and much closer to the way things are actually operating. The analogy that best suits us now has actually been in use for some time. Fortunately, Taoist wisdom is widely available to the West these days, and we now understand it without the need for a series of prerequisites, because Taoism is actually speaking what is to us our new language—the language of relativity, of interdependence, of the mutual interpenetration of everything that happens.

This new analogy and associated language are what make a new form of civilizing technology possible. You could also call it a *naturalizing* technology, because the foundations of our current technology first entered the scene as an outright barbarian—albeit a highly competent barbarian, all steely and glittery with a great force of arms. This forceful sort of technology is clearly not preferable, because it is rapidly transforming the face of the earth into its own image, which is the image of a machine.

We might be able to cover the earth with concrete, but good technologists know that our freeways will become obsolete at some point in the not-so-distant future, and grass will grow up through the cracks, and our roads will eventually vanish, because we shall take to the air like insects. And all of our wires and cables will likewise disappear, because we shall be able to transmit electricity without them. We shall abandon telephones as well, and the whole mechanical structure will vanish because it was only a step—only a peduncle. When a globule—let's say an amoeba or maybe a spot of oil suspended in water—begins to separate from the main body, it forms a sort of protrusion similar to a long neck. That extension will eventually break off, separate entirely from the main body, and form its own globule, leaving behind no trace of connection between the first body and the second. This is called the law of peduncles, and it explains all sorts of things—for example, why it's so difficult to find missing links in the evolutionary process.

{ We need to think of entirely new
political ideas . . . that embrace the
organic model of the universe. }

So all of these technological contraptions we've devised are all peduncles soon to vanish. At some point we won't even need houses because we'll know how to alter the temperature of the air or all live under an invisible plastic dome, and we'll no longer need to congregate in cities or travel, and everything we'd ever wish to know or learn will be available on a screen right in front of us.

Moving in this direction, however, requires the new analogy, and the people who are responsible for technical development need to be imbued with a more ecological philosophy or else we'll simply perpetuate mechanical anachronisms. The automobile, for example, is a hopeless anachronism with a gasoline engine that's going to prove difficult to get rid of because people will always be invested in selling oil. It's terribly difficult for an entire industry to change, but unless we make it happen, we will be stuck with anachronisms that blind us to ingenuity and our ability to see what actually needs to be done.

Some people might be alarmed by this way of talking and say that it sounds communistic. That's not what I'm suggesting at all. First of all, there's nothing more anachronistic than bureaucracy. The collective estate is a monolithic machine that is impervious to change because nobody has any responsibility. Just look at the communist countries today—they have just as tough a time as we do producing any worthwhile innovations.

We need to think of entirely new political ideas—ideas that have never been heard of but that embrace the organic model of the universe. The world is one body, but a body is a highly diversified system with divisions of function that still work as one. It's a lot more differentiated than an anthill. As opposed to a machine with a particular governor and parts that can be disassembled, replaced, and reordered, all of the parts of an organism work together in orderly anarchy. They govern themselves because an organism is something that functions without requiring external control.

Working with the Field of Forces

As discussed earlier, the Taoists felt that it was wise to exercise restraint when it comes to interfering with nature. In some situations, humans should keep their hands off things entirely; in others, humans should act by collaborating with nature, but only by taking into account the field of forces in which they are situated. Of course, we ourselves are that field of forces.

Realizing that we are the field of forces can be a sensuous experience, and it's one that can prove difficult to define and describe for two reasons: First, it's too complicated; second, you can't define the ground of reality. The continuum of all things can't be thought about as an object because you can't classify it. Even though it's tremendously important to know that you are it, you can't really say anything meaningful about that experience, but, on the other hand, not knowing the real you will make you go crazy. You become dementedly absorbed in details trying to identify yourself purely as this temporal and arbitrary role that you're playing, all the while forgetting that whatever happens in this round doesn't ultimately matter. In truth, to the field of forces in play, there are no winners and losers.

So how can we come to know that we are the field of forces in which we live? How do we know which way the wind is blowing so that we can sail properly? It isn't as simple as wetting your finger and holding it up to see which side gets cold first. Or is it?

We think that nature is extraordinarily complicated and therefore difficult to understand. And we think that if we can't understand our complicated situation, then it's immensely difficult to make decisions about it. From a different point of view, nature isn't complicated at all. When Buddhists speak about the world of form and the world that is formless, those two categories roughly correspond to the world that is complicated and the world that is simple.

What makes the world complicated isn't its actual physical structure but our attempts to understand it in a certain way. When we ask how something works—a flower, the human body, a geological structure—what we're really asking is how we can reproduce what's going on in words or numbers. Doing so, we can predict what it will do next and therefore exercise some degree of control. But the trouble with words and numbers is that they have peculiar limitations. It takes time to read or scan a mathematical expression, and it takes even longer to listen to a recording, and these expressions are like things strung out on a line requiring careful thought in order to understand the various steps that have been taken. These are methods for breaking down the phenomena of nature into code, and although the latest breakthroughs in computational technology can handle code at astonishing speed, the conscious mind can only process code slowly; it can only work in verbal and mathematical symbols, and those are quite clumsy.

By the time we have thoroughly thought about something, it's usually too late to do anything about it. The circumstances have changed in the meantime. The crisis about which we had to make a decision has already occurred. Therefore, we have to act without the kind of preparation we think we ought to have and without the kind of knowledge we think we ought to have, because we can't comprehend the world in real time in verbal and mathematical patterns. As a result, we feel frustrated. We think we're supposed to comprehend the world in symbols and manage it that way, but it should be obvious that there never will be a satisfactory explanation in terms of words because you can talk about the simplest object in the world forever and still not fully describe its attributes, as my earlier example of the Taoists making fun of the Confucians illustrates.

Words have a use, of course, but they only have that use when they are operating in subordination to a kind of organic understanding that doesn't depend on words at all. Words are like claws on the end of an arm—the claws are no good unless they are subordinate to the more subtle organization of the arm and the rest of the body. Words are the claws we use to tear life to pieces and arrange it in certain ways, just as we have to bite and chew apart our food in order to break it down into digestible pieces.

To make the world comprehensible, we have to claw it apart. But there are a lot of other acts of understanding we perform that are not contained in words—someone listening to you speak will engage in a number of nonverbal operations in order to get your point, and reading the words in a book necessitates the nonverbal facility of sight. It's impossible to put all of those functions into words. If your bathtub drain is clogged and you need to remove the water from the tub, you don't use a fork to do so because it would take forever. Instead, you use a pail. Describing the world in words is rather like trying to move water with a fork.

Words are only able to communicate to those who already know what you mean—"For unto every one that hath shall be given." And for that reason words are convenient because we can remind each other of things that we already know. As a word, *water* means nothing to a person who hasn't experienced water; it's only useful afterward as a form of shorthand. I can conveniently discuss water with this person now without having to bring some into the room and show it to them.

{ You know intelligence when you see it, even if it is something that in words escapes definition. }

In the same way, we use money instead of barter. Words have the same advantages and disadvantages as money. Money helps us to transfer wealth, and words help us to organize experience and communicate about it with each other. Beyond that, we run into insuperable difficulties when we try to describe our experience in words and through words attempt to comprehend the experiences of others. They're simply limited tools when it comes to understanding the field of forces in which we find ourselves.

Not too long ago, there were members of the Harvard faculty who were conducting some interesting experiments regarding different states of consciousness, and these faculty members were criticized by another professor at the university who said that no knowledge is academically respectable unless it can be put into words. I wonder what he thinks about everything going on in the departments of physical education, fine arts, and music. Unfortunately, a lot of people feel that way, especially members of the scientific and technological communities.

This takes us back to the earlier issue of the nature of intelligence. Intelligence is clearly not just verbal or computational. The eyes, our internal organs, and the organization of a plant are all obviously intelligent, and I say *obviously* because it should be obvious to anyone paying attention. You know intelligence when you see it, even if it is something that in words escapes definition, just as the nervous system is an undoubtedly intelligent organism that defies the comprehension of even the most learned neurologist. We know intelligence because it is fascinating, ingenious, wonderfully organized, and beautiful. We see it everywhere in the field of forces, in the patterns of nature, and in our fellow humans. Just look at us—the beauty of our eyes, the marvelous organization and coordination of our limbs, and so on. As Hamlet says, "What a piece of work is man! how Noble in Reason? how infinite in faculty? in form and moving how express and admirable? in Action, how like an Angel? in apprehension how, like a God? the beauty of the world, the Paragon of Animals!" All of this is us, even if we don't know how we are the way we are and do the things we do.

In the makeup of your nervous system and in the organization of the rest of your body, you are expressing a kind of intelligence that is—when looked at from the point of view of conscious analysis—unthinkably complex. And yet, from its own point of view, it's perfectly simple. You don't have to make an effort to see; you just see. You don't have to make an effort to hear; the ear does it for you. You don't have to make an effort to hold yourself together because your body already holds everything in place. You might have to exert yourself consciously in order to obtain food, keep warm, and occasionally defend yourself, but these efforts are only possible by innumerable processes you never have to think about—your heart, for example, continues to beat and circulate blood throughout your body without your deciding to make it do so.

Trust

It's a good thing that we don't have to make a decision about every single thing our body does. For one thing, there's nothing more exhausting than having to make one conscious decision after the other, and decisions are regularly accompanied by a peculiar anxiety. Did I make the right decision, the best decision? There's actually no way of knowing. You might think you know after the fact, but you never know before or during because you never know how much information you need to collect in order to make the right decision or whether or not the information is relevant to the decision at hand. Furthermore, every possible decision can be radically affected by unforeseeable variables.

Let's say you have just completed a business contract with a certain corporation and everything seems in order, but you had no way of knowing that the president of that corporation—upon whom the whole thing depends—is going to slip on a banana peel and injure his head in a serious accident. Who could have foreseen that eventuality? What could you have done—take out an insurance policy that included the possible danger of banana peels? How comprehensive would you have made the policy? How would you know that you weren't simply wasting money paying the premium?

And this is the anxiety with which we are faced. In trying to conduct our lives by the exercise of conscious will and control, we should realize that it is actually beyond our comprehension. We have no way of understanding everything we need to understand, because it is beyond us to foresee all possible eventualities. Trying to control things the way we do leads to a type of existence marked by an ongoing sense of frustration, and for thousands of years people have called this the *Fall*. The idea is that we have fallen away from a Golden Age, that something essential has been lost—an ancient, universal, and preferred way of being. At one point in the past, things supposedly went in accordance with the course of nature—what some people call the Tao.

The idea of the Fall is to blame for a good amount of preaching throughout history. Unfortunately, preaching rarely does anybody any good—it only creates more hypocrites. If I tell you that you ought to be concerned, that you ought to be unselfish, that you ought to cooperate, that you ought to be responsible, and so on, I'm implying that you are not. So we begin with a relationship marked by your resentment toward me for telling you that, and you will additionally most likely feel guilty because you are under the impression that you are indeed a separate self with the power to perform all of these virtues. Then you might go through the motions of doing what I tell you to do in my sermon, with disastrous results.

You remain an egocentric and selfish person, only now you are pretending that you aren't one. But the truth will always come out in the long run, and you will let down all the people who are relying on you to be someone whom you are pretending to be but whom you actually aren't. We have the most subtle ways of letting people down, all while going through the motions of doing exactly what they expect of us, and then we take it out on them when we feel forced into doing things that are against our own nature. We do all of this invariably, but we do our best to avoid being conscious of the ways in which we do it because that would puncture the whole balloon and show it for what it is—a farce. And we can't afford that.

Throughout it all, we know that there's a different way of being, and that's truly the source of our nostalgia for some sort of Golden Age. We have the feeling that once upon a time—maybe in our childhood, maybe back when we were in our mother's womb, or maybe way back in our evolutionary history before the invention of language and writing and numbers—things were fundamentally different and in accord with nature. We contemplate the animals around us and see that they don't seem to worry very much. They don't labor through decision-making processes—they just follow their nature. Whatever they do comes as naturally to them as when we sneeze or breathe or blink. It just happens.

So, we wonder, could it be possible for us to conduct our own lives that way? Instead of making one pathetic decision after another on the basis of utterly incomplete information, wouldn't it be possible to simply manage to do the right thing? To respond appropriately within the field of forces in which we are living? To no longer be restricted and frustrated by our own clumsy attempts to do everything by force and will?

The Taoists would say that there is, in fact, a way of living like this. The problem is that nobody will believe it, mostly because they're scared out of their wits that it won't work. But it should be obvious that if you are organically intelligent enough to be able to see without conscious effort, there's at least a faint possibility that the kind of intelligence that enables you to perform the incomprehensible operation of sight might also be of use in solving other problems, namely, those pertaining to a different way of being.

Instead of thinking of the human brain strictly as something one flexes and employs like a muscle, we could view it more as a network of neurological operations that are never truly conscious because we don't have to attend to them in detail. Only a tiny portion of thinking involves verbal processes. It's mostly a highly organized physical operation that's only complex when we try to describe it in words, because thinking itself happens quite naturally—it's the simplest thing in the world.

So if we are to adapt ourselves to the increasingly troublesome environment we are currently creating for ourselves, might we do so by trusting ourselves in a different way and using our capabilities to their fullest in order to come to an understanding of our problems? Of course, but it takes revising our view of ourselves.

We are not an ego in control of things who lives inside this bag of skin that bosses the bag around in the same way that a chauffeur in charge of a particular car does. That might be a useful analogy if we knew how the whole thing is constructed, but the whole point is that we don't. But if we could instead understand that we are the field of forces we find ourselves in, with all of their patterning and incredible intelligence, we could trust ourselves to simply respond spontaneously to situations as they occur. Instead, we have this continual anxiety about doing the right thing because we have been brought up in a civilization inured to the doctrine of original sin, which means that we cannot possibly trust ourselves.

Airline pilots are people and are therefore fallible beings. They are in charge of this enormous jet, and things happen way too fast for them to process every detail with conscious decisions, so increasingly we put more automated decision-making devices into aircraft. However, the more we do so, the more pilots lose confidence in themselves because more and more they have no idea how the damn thing works.

In limited circumstances, we can do a rather good job of eliminating error by use of computers, because a computer is more like a nervous system than a linguistic system. Computers are able to deal with a large number of operations at once and synthesize them. Words can't do that. Just like the ones you are reading now, they go along one after the other in a single track. But the human brain is infinitely more sophisticated than any computer we can construct; it's just that we aren't using our brains in the correct way.

The funny thing about geniuses is that they usually can't explain why they are geniuses. They can't teach it to others. They might say that it takes a lot of hard work, and that's true, but hard work isn't the cause of genius. It's more a necessary accompaniment to the art. When I was a young boy in school—around the ages of seven, eight, and nine years old—I was considered stupid because I always failed my examinations and received terrible marks. At the same time, I was absolutely fascinated with books—I absolutely loved them. I collected them, I read them, and I loved their smell and appearance, but nobody truly conveyed their purpose to me. I was always looking elsewhere to do better in school, but I didn't know how, so I studied the available exemplars of intelligence—some of the teachers I admired at school—and I believed I could become intelligent by imitating them: copying their handwriting, the way they wore their clothes, their gestures, their manner of speaking, and so on. It was as if I believed that by some sort of sympathetic magic I would acquire the mysterious power that I seemed to lack.

{ We have been brainwashed to believe in original sin, which says that the unconscious cannot be trusted. }

In a similar way, all of the nurses I encountered during childhood seemed to have a peculiar anxiety about constipation. They insisted that you do your duty (as they called it) every day, and if you did not perform accordingly, there was a graduated series of punishments, because the primary criterion of health seemed to be solely about not being constipated. First they'd give you a concoction called California syrup of figs. If that didn't work, they'd give you senna tea. Then it progressed to cascara and, if necessary, to castor oil, which is truly disgusting stuff. The trouble is that when they resort to all of that, your intestinal tract becomes so upset that you actually do become constipated and the whole thing starts all over again.

These solutions to their given problems are obviously not helpful. The primary mistake in them is the tendency to issue a commandment to the conscious mind to achieve a result that the conscious mind is perfectly incapable of producing. The conscious mind has nothing to do with whether you are constipated. That's the job of the unconscious, although I prefer to call it the superconscious because it's a lot more clever than the conscious mind is, as well as a great deal more trustworthy. But we have a hard time buying that because we have been brainwashed to believe in original sin, which says that the unconscious cannot be trusted. And if it wants to take a day or so off before going to the bathroom, we think there's something sinful going on—there's something wrong with it.

The attitude reflected in this rather trivial illustration runs through everything. It epitomizes our habitual way of being. And we've all been hypnotized to believe and promote these particular messages—*You must be good*, *You must be free*, *You must make the right decisions*, and so on. Well, as a result of those messages, we typically respond in one of two ways: We either lose our nerve or resolutely smash our way through existence. In the first response, we understand what's expected of us and realize that it's just too much—we simply can't make the right decisions—and so we turn our back on the whole thing and drop out. In the opposite response, we grit our teeth, pull ourselves together, and do what it takes to get rewarded accordingly. We perform as expected, we gain more and more power, and everything appears to be going great. The problem is that problems are endless. There's always something else to think of, something else to fix or control. And because we can't think about everything all at once, we have to turn things over to other intelligences—computers, for example.

Regardless of these other sources of intelligence, there's still a person at the center of it all who thinks they're in charge with their conscious intellect, and this person gradually feels more and more responsible. Just imagine being the president of the United States. You don't know what you're doing. You have all these decisions to make. You no longer have a private life because you're surrounded by telephones and the Secret Service and secretaries and so on, and whatever you choose to do doesn't make the slightest bit of difference to anything. Everybody objects. Everybody has a critique. Everybody calls you names. And the only way of insulating yourself from all of that is to try another approach and drop out, plug your ears, and what have you.

So you're stuck. But this is what happens to anybody who tries to play God in the wrong way. In actuality, everybody is God, so there's no need to try to be. The moment that anybody tries to be God, it means that they are doing so from the standpoint of a very limited faculty of conscious thinking and decision-making, and that's an entirely clumsy agency for controlling what happens in the world. You're never going to be God that way. What a nervous breakdown it would be if God had to think about every single motion that a gnat makes with its wings.

That's not an ideal way to be; it's not the best way to handle things. The way to handle things is the same way that the body does—it organizes itself without thinking about it. It has an intelligence, but it's not specifically linear or verbal. It's a multidimensional, multivariable intelligence in which everything is happening together all at once. And if we don't reacquaint ourselves with that kind of intelligence, we're going to be in trouble. It's already right here. We just have to give it a chance.

Synergy and the One World Town

Buckminster Fuller is a philosophical engineer, one of the most creative minds in the modern world.[2] His main claim to fame is inventing the geodesic dome, but beyond that he's done a great deal of fascinating thinking about the future of technology and the situation of our species in the universe. He also devised the term *synergy* from the Greek *sun* ("together") and *ergon* ("work").

What Fuller means by synergy is the fact that every complex organism as a whole entails an intelligence that exceeds the sum of its parts. Accordingly, he asserts that the industrial-natural complex in which we live is moving in a certain direction on its own, whether we like it or not. Fuller also says that this greater whole is able to organize your behavior in a more intelligent way than you can by yourself and that the increasing complexity of our world will of itself outlaw such things as the lunacy of war. Eventually, we will find ourselves progressively organized by an intelligent system that is not under our conscious direction yet still makes us feel as our individual selves feel inside our particular bodies.

All of the communications networks operating today—radio, television, telephone, and so on—constitute a type of global net, something akin to Teilhard's idea of the noosphere, *a sphere of thought encircling our planet that has evolved over time but is still very much a part of nature.* The *geosphere* is the material stuff that makes up the planet, the *biosphere* is the realm of living organisms atop the geosphere, and the biosphere in turn generates the noosphere, the communication network we call the mind.

As a result of the transportation network—specifically due to the advances in air traffic—all places in communication with one another are increasingly becoming the same place. If you fly to Tokyo from any other important city in the world, you might be slightly in doubt as to where you are because nowadays Tokyo is a mixture of Los Angeles, Paris, San Francisco, Shanghai, London, and other cities in Japan. Similarly, if you live in San Francisco, you realize it's becoming a lot more like Tokyo—people use chopsticks and tatami mats in their homes, cook over hibachi grills, and dine out at amazing sushi restaurants. You can also shop at supermarkets that sell all sorts of Japanese goods, not to mention items from India or Africa. In this way, how close you are to a given locale has simply become a matter of transportation. There are some places in the United States that take far longer for me to get to than, say, Tokyo.

In the past, it was the distance between places that made them different. When we use technology to get from one place to another faster and faster, the less worthwhile the actual place of arrival is because we've eliminated the distance between the two locations. If you take away the distance, then *there* is the same as *here*, and there's no point in going there in the first place. That's why I say there's no point in going to Honolulu anymore. It's the same place as here, for all intents and purposes. And there's certainly no point in flying from Los Angeles to Tokyo, other than a couple of nice little bars with great sushi, but you can get that in Los Angeles now, so it's practically the same place. Both have the same smog.

Regardless, there's a huge business in shuffling people all around the earth—planes are expensive and must be kept flying constantly. And one curious result of advances in the transportation network is that it is becoming increasingly more difficult for politicians and other parties to maintain an interest in starting and continuing wars with other countries. Even now, most of our wars are merely experimental. They occur in confined areas against people who allegedly don't matter, very much in order to test military materials and techniques, and these practices are all carefully arranged. However, these practice wars increasingly arouse passions and disturb people in all directions, because it turns out that there are no such things as unimportant people, and even these minor wars are becoming increasingly difficult to carry on. This is one of the reasons that Fuller is so hopeful about the future. He believes that synergy—the quality of intelligence of the total system—will overcome the ire of individuals, the troublesome parts that are unable to act with a full understanding of what's going on.

He also predicts the eventual arrival of a one world town. As you can see, it's happening quite fast. The speed of this transition is difficult for us to adapt to, just as when an elevator drops too fast or when we fly to London and still feel like our mind is back in San Francisco. It takes some time for us to catch up because all of our physiological rhythms get thrown off, and we as individuals are clearly having trouble grasping the larger picture, especially with the proliferation of information in today's world. Even committees of people have trouble organizing, controlling, and integrating all of this information, so imagine what it must be like for one person.

Privacy, Artificiality, and the Self

All of this innovation has many people worried, and a good number of them are concerned that the extension of the global network I'm speaking of—especially the electronic aspect of the network—might abolish individual privacy.

This topic comes up a lot in Marshall McLuhan's work.[3] McLuhan was the one who asserted that the wheel was a natural extension of our feet, that the carriage was a natural extension of the wheel, that the automobile was the same for the carriage, and so on. These progressive steps are all technological extensions of the human organism, and the electronic network that so many people are concerned about—telephones, radios, televisions, computers, and so on—is merely an extension of our nervous system.

Advancements in the electronic network are happening at an astonishing rate. Before you know it, we'll have boxes inside our homes with little screens on them that will enable us to key in a given code and access any book of our choosing in the Library of Congress, and we'll be able to do so at our own rate and pace. We'll also soon have the ability to arrange lasers in such a way as to create a three-dimensional image in color that we can project in a certain area and even walk around inside it. And when reproductions become so technically perfect in this way, we won't be able to tell the difference between the reproduction and the original. When you get phenomena like this, it raises the question of where a person actually is.

And then there's the question of who we are. Before long we'll be able to manufacture parts of the human body in perfect plastic so that when your heart or kidneys go wrong, a surgeon will simply replace them with a reproduction that works equally well. They might never be able to reproduce the brain, but surely they will be able to insert a device that connects to a computer system of some kind. And if your parts are replaced, are you the same individual that you once were?

{ The distinction between artificial
and natural is itself artificial. }

This process of replacement occurs naturally in your body, of course, just as it does in larger structures and institutions like the University of California. Even though the students, faculty, administration, buildings, and so on change constantly, we still recognize it as the University of California. The university is a pattern of behavior, and the organisms involved in that pattern keep changing while the pattern retains an identifiable continuity. It's the same with a whirlpool in a stream—the water is running through the pattern, and in a sense the whirlpool is never the same. What we call the University of California is the soul, and its bodily expression keeps changing. Similarly, we are all electronic echoes of ourselves. From the standpoint of physics, we are the most remarkable electronic patterns.

On psychedelics, some people have what's called a *plastic doll* experience, in which everything appears as if made from inorganic, cheaply made plastic. Others have an opposite experience, seeing everything as if it were living jewelry emanating a beatific inner light. In general, the plastic version is not as preferable. It suggests a diabolic vision, but it's often through the diabolic vision that you can gather the deepest insights. If you can go down into any experience—that is, if you can explore a certain sensation or feeling in order to find out all of its implications, regardless of whether or not you like and dislike those implications—you will find that the plastic doll type of experience allows for greater bliss and realization than merely exploring things that appear lovely at first sight.

We consider technology as an artificial sort of thing, but the reality is that nothing is artificial. I'd even go so far as to say that the distinction between *artificial* and *natural* is itself artificial and that the constructs of human beings are no more unnatural than the nests of birds and bees. As McLuhan says, our constructs are extensions of ourselves.

But what happens to our privacy when all of us become computerized and none of us are hidden? The telephone companies have a sort of regulation whereby you cannot simply switch your telephone off. You might be able to switch off a given extension in your home, but you are unable to switch off your main phone. If you leave it off the hook long enough, it will start screaming at you. Some people predict that it's only a matter of time until our ordinary telephones disappear and are replaced by individual devices about the size of a pocket watch—one side will have a TV screen and speaker; the other will entail a set of buttons you can use to activate various functions or dial world information for any given individual. And if that person doesn't answer, it will mean that they are dead. Under such circumstances, absolutely no one can get lost anymore.

We can see the law of peduncles in play everywhere. Railroads became increasingly obsolete with the advent of automobiles, and year after year there are fewer rusty old railroad tracks in existence. With the development of aircraft, roads are slowly becoming anachronistic, and the wires and connective fibers involved with all sorts of communication are also becoming obsolete. As new technology emerges, the connecting links of older forms disappear. At some point in the future, electronic communication will even take the place of air travel, because with the power of lasers I'll be able to re-create myself in front of my father in England, just as if I were sitting in the same room with him. We can conceive—as some science fiction writers already have—of a rather appalling situation in which we never need to leave our place of residence. Any food we need will be delivered automatically. What's the next step beyond that? Maybe we abolish food altogether and simply consume special essences, or undergo a type of electronic stimulation that does everything for us that food originally did.

At some point, the only peduncle remaining from what we have today will be the black box of electronic gadgetry. By that time, we'll have become so etherealized that we'll transition right into telepathy and psychic communication, which will mean that all privacy whatsoever will have vanished. Your thoughts will be easily read by anyone—your insides will be an open book. And this is what all properly educated Americans and all properly educated British dread most—the conversion of humanity into an anthill of the worst type.

In England we say that our home is our castle. Everybody needs a castle, a place where you can get away from it all and just be yourself. Let's say you have that.

Let's say that you're away from it all and you're inside your castle just being yourself. Well, unfortunately, you're there just being yourself with a lot of thoughts inside your head that aren't yours. You think in a language given to you by other people that contains their own ideas and prejudices, and there's nothing you can do to avoid that. Some Japanese people I know say that when they think in Japanese, they have certain feelings that are characteristically Japanese, but when they think and speak in English, they can no longer access the Japanese feelings.

If you have thoughts, you're already in the sphere of public influence. Your thoughts are delivered in a tone of voice that sounds a lot like your father or mother or aunt or schoolteacher or particularly opinionated friend who tells you who you are and how you ought to behave. In the dome of your skull, there's a pandemonium going on all the time—a myriad of voices and influences working upon you even when you are physically quite alone. You think these are your thoughts, but they're nothing of the kind. And that means you are not nearly as much of a private individual as you think. You're also exercising these influences upon other people. You're constantly telling them who they are, what you think about them and their behavior. And even if they don't believe you, they nevertheless pay serious attention to it. They can't help it.

B. F. Skinner liked to perform a terrifying experiment in which he sent two students (A and B, selected arbitrarily) out of the classroom. Then Skinner would tell the other students in the class to agree with everything that student A said and disagree with B entirely, and bring the two back in. And the result, of course, was that no matter their temperament, student A would become encouraged, built up, sprouting, and more articulate. Student B, on the other hand, would become baffled, confused, and uncomfortable. It's a drastic example of how we're colossally influenced by each other.

For this reason, I think that Harry Stack Sullivan's basic ideas about psychology and psychopathology are more profound than Freud's. Freud was always focused on individual history, physiology, and the interior of the individual, whereas Sullivan saw the individual as a particular expression of a social network. George Herbert Mead taught this, too. He called the conceptions that we have about ourselves the *generalized other*, which is the sum total of all the things people have told us we are because we can't know ourselves as a self outside the context of society. Just as we can't biologically exist without a father and mother, we cannot carry on an existence without a society. The reactions of others provide us with the mirror in which we attain self-realization. We only know who we are in terms of our relationships with others.[4]

So, back to the topic of privacy; we can contemplate the complete integration of human society from two different points of view: pro and con. On the positive side, there's no longer anything to hide, and we can give up all worries concerning ownership. If someone says they would like something of ours, we let them have it because we know very well that we can always go up to someone else and ask for something of theirs and receive it. Furthermore, nobody has any dirty little secrets anymore, so we can drop a lot of pretense and enjoy a fellowship with one another that has no barriers and defenses. We all cooperate dutifully and love each other. On the negative side, all people become basically the same individual. Perhaps that's what the Hindus mean when they say that we are all one, that we are all the Godhead in disguise.

Part of our difficulty in the first place is that we begin with a certain conception of what it means to be an individual person. In the Christian sense of *ego*, the soul is something alive, with consciousness and intelligence, that lies hidden somewhere in this bag of skin. As King John says to Hubert in Shakespeare's *The Life and Death of King John*, "Within this wall of flesh, there is a soul counts thee her creditor and with advantage means to pay thy love." See the image? The wall of flesh contains the soul. The castle contains the king. We're brought up to believe that we are a soul inside a body and that every soul that exists does so in infinite value in the eyes of God.

Ever since the Industrial Revolution, we have instituted a tremendous technological campaign to preserve the individual. All kinds of social services, hospitals, ambulances, medicines, welfare agencies, and so on are dedicated to preserving life, to helping us live longer and longer, and to giving us what's called a full opportunity to develop our personality. This type of thinking was almost unthinkable in Asia until we exported our methods of industrialization and sanitation and the message that every single person is an individual to be loved and cherished and treated properly because each particular human organism is infinitely precious. The great humanitarian movement of the nineteenth century was based on this belief, and people like John Wesley and Charles Dickens and Archibald Foss and so on dedicated their lives to rescuing the precious individual from the ravages of impersonal disease and political exploitation.

Ever since American capitalist liberalism achieved the apex of this sort of ideal, we've become leery of anything else, especially when it comes to anything socialistic or communistic. Our theory of liberal capitalism in the United States is that the state is the servant of the individual and that police, military, and governmental officials of all types are under our employ in order to serve us. We call them public servants, and we remind them from time to time that it is we who pay their salary. There's something aristocratic about that. And more and more people feel that it is beneath their dignity to be in a service role to others, say, as a waiter or barber. And being a shoe shiner is considered a terrible thing, because shoes are on the feet, which are as low down as you can go—you might as well be kissing people's feet while you're at it. Anything that involves material service skills is denigrated, so some of these job titles in the name of equality have changed into something more noble and professional. Undertakers are now morticians; janitors work for maintenance services. Maybe barbers will start calling themselves tonsorial technicians.

There's another example I've personally been irritated by, and that's the use of first names by strangers. Maybe it's my British snobbiness, but I get irritated when the guy at the garage sees my credit card and addresses me as "Al." This level of familiarity is extraordinarily common, especially in California, and I personally became distinctly uncomfortable when I found myself on first-name terms with my boss, who happened to be the president of the University of the Pacific. The reason I felt uncomfortable was that the whole thing felt insincere. He and I didn't have a first-name relationship, and the use of first names between us was only an effort to prove that there really ought to be that sort of relationship between us when neither of us had any intention of forming one. From the outside, the practice is quite baffling.

Ironically, what we can see in this sort of practice is a creeping socialism—the dreaded abolition of everything that is individually precious and private. The boundaries are disappearing, and we as a collection of individual human beings seem to be dissolving into an amorphous mass. We have a great fear of that because we've witnessed the degree to which people can be controlled when they disappear into an amorphous mass—Hitler's legions, for example, or the identically uniformed waves of Chinese troops.

These are drastic examples of the eradication of individualism and privacy. Usually, attacks to our privacy are more mundane and psychological. For example, we're sitting at the bar next to a drunk who fancies themselves an expert or psychological guru of some sort. They invade our privacy by refusing to play by the usual social rules whereby we communicate with each other without actually saying anything at all, for example, "How are you?" "Fine, thank you." "Nice day, isn't it?" and so on. We use these little social platitudes to feel each other out and determine the boundaries of our relationships, but some people don't play along—they invade our privacy by refusing the game, maybe to one-up us or see how uncomfortable they can make us.

When people invade our privacy in these ways, there are multiple tactics of response at our disposal. For example, you could ask, "Didn't your mother ever teach you manners?" or simply shrug or say nothing at all. Krishnamurti does that. If you make a comment about somebody in his presence that is in any way adverse or critical, he'll give no response at all. It's like tossing a rock into a well and waiting for a splash that never comes.[5] On the other hand, there are people like Allen Ginsberg, who—if anybody presses him too hard or invades him in whatever way—will just strip down naked. It's as if he's saying, "Okay, if you want to challenge me, then I'll choose the weapons." And there's a marvelous feeling to that—it doesn't feel like he has anything to hide whatsoever. If you're stark naked, you can't depend on material gimmicks for your personal worth—not your clothes, not your car, not your watch or fountain pen, not your home. So confronting people in an atmosphere of physical or spiritual nakedness can utterly disarm anyone trying to keep up an accustomed role. Of course, stripping down won't work that way with me, because being naked won't prevent me from talking and defending myself with language.

If you have nothing to lose, you don't really fear anything. That being said, there are some truly degraded ways in which we deprive people of their individualization and privacy—people forced to live in prisons and mental hospitals, for example. In such places, there are no corners or secrets. The bathrooms are completely exposed, and everybody is herded around in the same uniform and the same haircut, much as they do in the military. The idea is to degrade the individual ritually so that they are brainwashed into becoming an obedient tool of the system. But then what do we end up with? Monarchical politics again, because it doesn't matter whether the system that controls people in that way is headed by an individual monarch or a totalitarian state. It makes no difference.

Groups and Crowds

This brings us to the difference between groups and crowds. This distinction is key to getting around the things that seem threatening in a society in which there is no privacy. A crowd consists of a number of identical individuals, suitably brainwashed by a leader. Again, it doesn't matter whether the leader is an individual or a bureaucratic entity of some kind. The crowd and the leader are not actually in communication with each other. For example, when a politician speaks to an enormous audience, that audience is a crowd of individuals who mostly don't know each other, and the communication moves only in one direction. The politician speaks at the crowd, and they can't truly answer back unless they do so as a group, as in "*Sieg Heil!*" They can only reply as a collective.

{ *It's a lot harder to bamboozle a group of people who are in communication with one another.* }

A group, on the other hand, has a contrasting design. A group has no particular leader, because the group itself is an organism. The lines of communication in a group are multidimensional—they run all over the place. Because of this, an effective group of human beings is one in which there aren't too many people because everyone knows each other and is able to live in communication with each other. When the group gets too large, subgroups form, and each subgroup appoints a representative to communicate with the representatives of the other subgroups. This, of course, was the original design for the Republic of the United States.

The problem arises when this arrangement transforms into a hierarchy of cell structures in which the members of the various subgroups are no longer in communication with each other. It simply becomes too complicated for any one person to keep track of. For this reason, in the United States there is an enormous difference between a given individual and an electoral representative, who is the one actually responsible for electing the president. Individual members of the group gradually know less and less, and their involvement with the overall running of things decreases as well.

It's the easiest thing in the world to bamboozle an enormous number of people by mass persuasion and get them to do practically anything you want. All dictators vote themselves into office by referendum. But it's a lot harder to bamboozle a group of people who are in communication with one another. A monolithic state is utterly paternalistic, whereas a tribal community is something else entirely. However, a tribe has to be small enough to maintain and promote this type of discussion—not voting but establishing a consensus through discussion. Native Americans and Quakers alike know that voting is an unreasonable procedure. Unlike crowds, groups get together and sort things out.

It's also easy to fool people into believing they're a group as opposed to a crowd. It's common, for example, for people at home all over the United States to be watching the same television program in a sort of great national hookup. And the more we develop microelectronic machinery, the greater the capacity for this is, because programs are rapidly becoming easier to produce, run, broadcast, and receive in better quality at home. Furthermore, there's a growing offering of material on an increasing number of electronic channels. McLuhan says that the point of all of this has everything to do with our exposure to and involvement in a televised medium.

When we plug in through media, we get turned on by what appears to be a huge in-and-out of human communication of all sorts. It's not the same thing, of course, because when you touch someone physically, you communicate with them directly. Just the act of touching can send a message of affection or love. People love to wander the streets and mingle with interesting crowds of other people who are shopping or just walking around back and forth, not saying anything to them but enjoying an exciting feeling of being involved with others and their colorful goings-on.

Television can lead us to think of ourselves like the old Italian peasant woman who watches the busy world pass by outside her windowsill—there seems to be something fundamentally good about it, something we can associate with colorful villages, exciting streets, and the romance of an archaic peasant person. And observing the ever-varying panorama of life is not completely excluded by electronic technology as long as people are organized in a group—a true net. But this is not a true net; it's just a trap.

3

Money and Materialism

Until we get over our particular hang-up of the hallucination of separateness, it will be difficult to form a new relationship with money, our possessions, and the material present. Ignoring the inseparability of all things goes hand in hand with a bad or inadequate relationship with the material present, and there never is anything but the present. I say the material present because it is crucial to understand that the present moment is where we have always lived and where we will always live and that there is no other time than right now. The past and future are only abstractions.

But we mustn't think of the present as a split second, as if we're looking at the second hand on our watch, because that's just an abstract view. Watchmakers make those lines as small as visibly possible, and the second hand sweeps across them so quickly that you hardly have time to say "now," and we've come to think of that slice of time as the present moment, but it's not. Present time is more like an oval-shaped field of vision with a clear center and fuzzy edges. When you're listening to music, you don't hear it one note at a time—you hear it in phrases, you anticipate what's coming, and you recall what has already been played. That's the wide but fuzzy-edged view of what is called the present.

In this culture, we aren't brought up to see that, which has something to do with why we live for the future. We live for the future mainly because our present is inadequate, and our present is inadequate because we are not seeing it fully. We see it only in terms of abstractions. That's why we're always looking into the future for something else, something more—more life, more time, more whatever it is—because one of these days it will all be all right, and the thing we're looking for will hopefully happen. Of course, it never does. Not if you live that way. Because when you attain all your goals in life and rise to the top of your profession and have your beautiful spouse and children, you still feel the same as you've always felt. You're still looking for something in the future, and there isn't any future—not really. So only people who live in proper relationship with the material present have any use for making any plans at all, because then if the plans work out, they're actually capable of enjoying them. But if you aren't fully here and your mind is always off somewhere else, you'll remain starved and always rushing to get someplace else. And there's nowhere to go except here.

Our schools don't prepare us to relate to the material present. Instead, we're educated to become bureaucrats, accountants, lawyers, and doctors, who are all good at making money, which is said to be incredibly important. And the children who aren't considered fit for the college education that these careers require are encouraged to take reluctantly offered courses in trades and manual skills. You hear these jokes about being able to receive your bachelor's degree in basket weaving from any American university, but that would actually be an improvement on our current state of affairs. The larger point is that we are encouraged to become obsessed with the life of abstractions, with problems of status, and with problems of the world *as* symbolized rather than the world *to be* symbolized. This explains our hang-ups when it comes to money. When it comes down to it, most of us are incapable of relating directly to physical existence at all.

The Material Is the Spiritual

The World Congress of Faith was held in London in 1936. Sarvepalli Radhakrishnan, Yusuf Ali, D. T. Suzuki, and many other famous scholars and experts were in attendance, and at the final meeting of the congress they took over the Queen's Hall, which was a giant auditorium. The subject matter for the evening was "The Supreme Spiritual Ideal," and representatives from all of the world's religious traditions got up and delivered volumes upon volumes of hot air. Suzuki was the final speaker.

He said something like "I'm feeling confused tonight. I'm a simple country person from a faraway place, and I find myself in this assembly of learned people. I'm supposed to talk about supreme spiritual ideas, but I don't know what that means, so I looked up *spiritual* in the dictionary, but I don't understand. Spiritual is supposed to be on one side and material world on the other, but both to me are unreal." And then he went on to describe his house and garden in Japan at great length.

When he was finished, he received a standing ovation. He was real. He came across as lovable and intelligible and human, as distinct from a mere preacher. And his point was intensely important—if you understand the spiritual correctly, it isn't different from what we call the material.

{ *What is spiritual has nothing whatsoever to do with abstractions.* }

As a word, *material* is misinterpreted. We can use the word to apply to our body, the earth, rocks, trees, animals, and all that, and we set that kind of material aside as something quite different from the spiritual or the mental, which we view as some kind of vaguely gaseous realm that permeates the material world. Or instead of gaseous it's abstract—a world of ideas, a world of principles. This division is curious and debasing, however, because the material and spiritual domains of life have vitality only when they're together.

When you see the material in the spiritual and the spiritual in the material, both of these concepts tend to vanish. When you have an immediate, aware relationship with the present, your vision of the material world is transformed, and you see that it isn't material and it isn't spiritual—it is indefinable. It's what there is, and there's no way of describing that. You can't put it into any particular category, and you can only find what you can classify.

The material is the spiritual, but in order to understand that, we have to distinguish between the material and the abstract, making sure that we don't confuse the abstract with the spiritual. The abstract world is one of symbols, words, and concepts, and it has the same relationship to the physical universe as a menu does to a dinner or as money does to wealth. What is spiritual has nothing whatsoever to do with abstractions—it's actually a lot closer to what we call physical reality or the material world.

The correct use of the word *material* means something more like "metered" or "measured." When we say that something is *immaterial*, it means that it doesn't matter—that is to say, it doesn't measure up to anything. The measured world—the world as represented in pounds, miles, decibels, photons, or whatever—is, of course, abstract, because when you measure the world, you don't really make any difference to it. What we deem the equator doesn't actually cut the world in two pieces.

What is the world upon which we impose our measurements? You can point to it, but you can't really say what it is. It's not a *what*, but it's the world we're actually living in, what Alfred Korzybski calls the *unspeakable world*. So when I refer to the material present, I don't mean the measured present but the physical present of actual nonverbal being.

People who do not relate well to the material present—the physical present—become incompetent in the practical arts of life. They become bad cooks, bad lovers, bad architects, bad potters, bad clothiers, and so on because they really have no love for anything except abstractions—quantities, money, status, and symbols. People are so bamboozled by symbols that they want the symbol more than they want what it signifies. But if you want what is signified by the symbol, then you've got the universe by the tail because everything that is symbolized by a symbol is inseparable from the whole universe.

When you catch a fish, it's not just a thing called a fish that you have. You are being fed by the ocean and everything that goes with the ocean. You are being sustained by this colossal life, just as if the ocean reached out and fed you. That's the real reason for giving thanks at meals. Some people thank God, but it's a more concrete expression of gratitude to thank the fish, but then you have to thank the ocean and so on.

When most of us talk about the physical world, we often think of it in a derogatory way. However, when theologians talk about the *evils of the flesh*, we're not talking about the physical body as much as we are a conception of the body as something to be exploited in order to satisfy one's spiritual emptiness. So, too, when we speak of materialism, we aren't really talking about materialism. Instead, what we're referring to is an abstract conception of the value of the material world. Real materialism would be the love of material things, and that's quite a bit different from the materialism that we actually see in practice. If you truly get in touch with your senses and the so-called physical world, you're in for a lot of pleasant surprises.

One of our problems in the West is that we think about the relationship between the spiritual and the physical by the analogy of form and matter, in which a pot is the form made from the matter of clay. We can't put the two together, because we're hung up on a conception of matter as a type of primordial stuff, and this stuff has neither intelligence nor energy. That's why when we think of the world in terms of form and matter coming together, we have to evoke an external agency that informs matter, brings it into shape and order, and produces art.

This is meaningless dualism. Nobody has ever seen immaterial form, just as nobody has ever seen formless material. What is this stuff out of which the universe is supposedly made? *Stuff* is actually a word for looking at the world with bad focus. When your focus on something isn't clear, it's fuzzy, and this fuzziness or indistinctness is what we call *stuff*. However, when your focus on the world is clear, you see patterns and details and structure. And when you look more closely into those patterns and structures, everything starts to get fuzzy again; until you turn up the level of magnification, and everything becomes clear again, and you see smaller patterns, details, and structures.

In this way, we always encounter the world as patterning—never as stuff—and so, in a sense, the physical world that surrounds us is immaterial. It's a fantastic pulsation of vibrations that gives an illusion of solidity, just as if I twirl a lit cigarette around in the dark, it appears that there's a continuous circle of light or fire. Just so, the apparent motion of the present moment from the past to the future gives the illusion of continuity, as if there were something extended in time. The table appears to be solid, but only because it vibrates with such tremendous energy. And so what we ordinarily conceive of as the material world is not what we think it is but instead is something intensely magical and strange.

As Spinoza once said, the more you know of particular things, the more you know of God. If you want to find out about Buddha-nature, about Brahman, about what is spiritual, the best thing to do is to go directly to the physical world and find out.

Money and the Good Life

The fact that we in the West are obsessed with abstract attainments goes back to curious factors in our history regarding money and caste. You might already be familiar with the castes originating in ancient India, the Brahmins (priests, theologians, and intellectuals), Kshatriyas (warriors and rulers), Vaishyas (farmers and merchants), Shudras (blue-collar workers), and Dalits (the untouchables). We don't like to admit it, but these castes are perennial—that is, they still exist in our societies today. You've got professors and businesspeople and laborers and your typical American fraternity sort with his crew cut who loves alcohol and football and so on. It's all there.

In the sixteenth century, something curious happened in Europe during the Reformation—the Vaishyas got the upper hand on the Brahmins and Kshatriyas. The feudal aristocracy began to lose power to the great merchant bankers of Italy and the burghers of Central Europe, and the Roman Catholic Church began to lose power because its doctrine was criticized and fell under increasing suspicion. Protestantism was a creation of the burgher cities of Europe—places like Geneva, Frankfurt, London, Edinburgh, and so on. As a consequence, money values began to dominate Christian theology. The number of holy days were cut down by all Protestant sects because the merchants didn't want their workers taking all of these holidays off. The Protestant ethic places great value on the virtues of saving and frugality, which are essentially Vaishya ideas run wild.

This is where the United States inherited its basic conception of the good life. It's largely the creation of bourgeois Protestantism, which is why we have a bad relationship with the material present. Our whole world is based on two contradictory ideas: First, save up; put your money aside and invest it. Second, happiness comes from buying things.

When people feel inadequate, bored, or unfulfilled, a great number of them try to rid themselves of the sensation by spending their money. Some people even use the entire day to go shopping—it's considered the thing to do. Go out and shop all day and come home loaded with all kinds of things. Unfortunately, these things are not true material possessions—most of them are poorly made, and you can't use so many things in your home in the first place. You can store them and show them to your friends, but even if you own six houses, you can only live in one at a time. And it's the same with horses or cars—unless you're performing some sort of circus act, you can only ride one at a time. Even so, we tend to become absolutely overloaded with possessions and have difficulty moving around, because every time we move we have to carry all this heavy stuff with us—oversized chairs and other huge things. They're the perfect pest—we have to use our muscles to lug them around, they have to be cleaned, and moths have to be kept out of them. And we call this material comfort.

Not all cultures have this hang-up. In a Japanese living room, you'll find a small table with some cushions on the floor, and instead of an enormous bed in the bedroom you'll have a futon that's delightful to sleep on. You don't have all of these vast objects you need to haul and push around. Westerners don't understand furniture; most of what we have in our homes is absolutely uninspired junk of poor design. It has nothing whatsoever to recommend it—it isn't fun at all. Our homes, too, are terrible. When you see the sort of shelter that most people in the United States have provided for themselves, you're aghast—miles and miles of these boxes that you wouldn't want a dog to live in.

Our addiction to abstract attainment shows up in our clothing as well. By and large, we are shockingly dressed when you compare what we wear with that of other cultures. Men here go around looking like funeral directors in the most uncomfortable survival wear that almost looks like military uniforms, and women wear frocks and dresses of no real joyous color that cover up these systems of pulleys and blocks and tackles. Of course, there are exceptions, but I'm talking about a culture in general that has chosen a style of clothing that doesn't look as if anybody enjoys wearing it.

We only wear what we wear because we are expected to be dressed, covered up, and decent, and so our clothes are worn apologetically. Most of our clothing is made of cloth as well, and when you weave cloth it comes out in long rectangular strips that have very little to do with the contours of the human body. That's why our jackets don't fold up properly, and whenever we take them out of a suitcase they require dry cleaning or ironing. Our shirts, too, are ridiculous constructions that become easily wrinkled and get filthy in nothing flat. Our neckties are virtual nooses. There's no rationale to them or any of this whatsoever.

The traditional style of dress in Japan is quite different. Their kimonos haven't been forced to fit the human body, and they therefore fit comfortably—the cloth conforms to you by its nature, thereby giving you a certain dignity.

The Tibetans have a method of pounding wool rather than weaving it, and they make these straightforward cloaks that are split down the center with a place at the sides for your arms to go. One evening four other men and I took turns trying one on, and it turned all of us into kings—we looked absolutely regal and dignified. In England, there are traditional tweeds from the Hebrides; Mexico has all of these colorful and gorgeous materials; India uses wonderful silk for saris and the like; and in Java you'll find beautiful batik for sarongs. Additionally, these materials last forever, and they're made by people with true enthusiasm for making them, mainly because in the lives of these people there isn't such a differentiation between work and play.

{ *Money isn't practical until you spend it and, more importantly, enjoy it.* }

For us, work and play are quite different. We work in order to make money to enjoy a good life and play. This is insane. We spend most of our time working jobs that we don't really value, and then we're supposed to come home and enjoy ourselves, except that we're too tired from work and we don't get around to playing unless it's a Saturday or some other day off. For many of us, evening play takes the form of sitting around and passively watching television. Compared to the people of India and Africa, we have all the money in the world—we live like royalty. But we don't. You'd think we'd celebrate and have parties and orgies and banquets all the time, but instead we live in a form of constant disappointment.

Living in Beverly Hills is apparently a sign of great wealth. Why? Why spend all that money to live in Beverly Hills when you can live someplace else without all of that poisoned air? Businesspeople like to imagine that they're practical—they'll say they don't believe in philosophy; they like action; they like to get things accomplished. Is that what it means to be practical? To make a lot of money and live in overpriced, ugly houses in crowded neighborhoods? Money isn't practical until you spend it and, more importantly, enjoy it. And it's quite difficult to enjoy money when you make a lot of it because you're afraid you're going to lose it. Somebody might take it all away. Lots of people think that if they had a little more money, their problems would be solved. But then they make a little more money—maybe even enough to move to Beverly Hills—and they immediately start worrying about their health. There is always something to worry about—always. And you can even make it worse by trying to accomplish and buy all of those things that are supposed to stop your worrying.

I should amend my earlier comments about Japan. Unfortunately, our attitudes toward work and clothing and far too much else have become contagious. I have a Japanese friend who always wears Western clothes in his country now. He wouldn't be seen dead in a kimono in Kyoto, and he primarily wears our style of clothing—that is, Western suits—because you can't very well run after a bus in a kimono. See, a kimono is not designed for rushing about—it's made for comfort and leisure. In a kimono, you have to stroll—you have to take it slow. And if you have to rush around and wear particular clothing that enables you to do so, it means that you are not relating to the material present very well.

True Materialism

This speeding about—this ridiculous hurry and forcefulness—shows up everywhere. In white Anglo-Saxon Protestant culture, for example, the food is unbelievably bad, and—similar to our approach to clothing—the only reason we eat it is because we have to. The result of this is that we think of food primarily from the point of view of abstract dietetics rather than taste, and whenever dietitians interfere with cooking, it gets utterly destroyed. It's as if the only important thing in food were nutritious chemicals. The problem with focusing on eating only what's good for us is that it's future oriented—we eat in such and such a way because it prolongs our life. But what's the point of going on and on into the future when all of the meals ahead of us are unappetizing things designed to enable us to go further into the future?

This entirely futuristic dietetic attitude to food reveals again our purely quantitative thinking and our lack of relationship to the material world. We wake up in a hurry, and so we have instant coffee, which doesn't taste like coffee. We rush the growth of tomatoes, and so they don't taste like tomatoes anymore. There's a type of apple called "Delicious," which isn't—it's nothing but wet pith. This way of relating to our food is, furthermore, entirely disrespectful to the creatures we have killed in order to eat, and if we don't respect our onions and fish and so on, we certainly won't cook them properly, which means that we'll enjoy our food even less.

We're constantly rushing after the thing, the result, the whatever-it-is that we thought we wanted. We convinced ourselves that it would make us happy. But having all of these things isn't doing it for us—it's supposed to, but it doesn't. We don't eat well, and we too often use food in order to feel happy, but instead we end up with obesity and indigestion.

Everywhere we look, advertisements persuade us that the most important thing in life is to buy a certain type of car, yacht, or house, but even if we can do so, we don't end up happy. And then we wonder why and feel cheated. All of this illustrates that we aren't *here*. That's close to what we say when someone is insane—we say that they're "not all there." For answers, we then go to a psychoanalyst, a priest, a support group, all of which persuade us in a different direction, but it always feels as if something's missing.

Nothing is missing. There's nothing missing at all—unless, of course, you're absolutely starving or freezing, which most of us aren't. When we are adequately fed and sheltered, there isn't anything missing. It's all there, only nobody is there to see it. Everybody is wandering off after something else in the distance.

Another important aspect to life is lovemaking. Here again, it's a subject neglected in Western education from any practical point of view, as opposed to, say, the brilliance of the *Kama Sutra*. We, too, could think of sex as enjoyable and fun and a great art that transpires between lovers, but instead we commit ourselves to it because it's supposedly good for us—it's a healthy outlet. And, of course, it's necessary for having children, which again are things for the future.

When we do have children, we also don't relate to them very well, and you see all of these fathers and mothers who feel guilty for one reason or another. Maybe their lives aren't turning out so great, but they hope their children will have it better, so they work even harder to earn a living for the sake of the children. And they live as wife and husband for the sole purpose of bringing up children. This is completely backward. If parents have vocations—that is to say, if they are interested in and devoted to their work—the children will also take an interest in that work, be it medicine or cooking. That would encourage children to actually want to help, which we typically don't allow them to do in this society because you can't possibly have children around the factory or office. In other societies, prior to schooling, children help out on the farm or in the shop alongside their parents and learn their crafts.

Instead, we propitiate our children with toys. Often these are fake plastic replicas of things that adults play with—guns, dolls, vehicles, and so on—and they never quite live up to expectations. The children break them and become furious, and every American home I know of in which there are children is strewn from end to end with disintegrating plastic. As a result, you have these screaming, knock-down/drag-out battles with parents trying to get children to clean up and throw away the mess that their parents bought them.

The whole family and work setup in our culture is an institution hanging over from agrarian civilization that just doesn't work in an urban-industrial civilization. We only keep it up because we think that's the way things are supposed to be, and we've never rethought human relationships in immediate relation to this new kind of situation in which we're living. For the most part, we come home from jobs in which nobody is interested, and we spend most of our time with people with whom we have no real relationship. There are, of course, families that thrive and get on reasonably well with each other, but they are fortunate flukes.

And poor women—throughout all of this, they're always having to live up to the image of some movie star or whoever is supposed to be the ideal type of the day. Our notions of feminine beauty are entirely fabricated by the curious creeps who edit *Vogue* and *Harper's Bazaar*. We set up these ideal external surface forms of beings that have no sensitivity to substance, weight, volume, temperature, or smell.

Among all matters of the material present, the most repressed in this culture is the sense of smell. Interestingly enough, smell is one of the main channels of unconscious communication, and a great deal of ESP, telepathic communication, and the intuitive likes and dislikes we form regarding other people are the result of smell, which we don't pay enough attention to. Usually when we use the word *smell* we mean something bad—"It smells"—and in English we typically think only in terms of three qualities of smell—fragrance, acridity, and pungency. All of the other adjectives used for smell are borrowed from taste or some other sense, because it's repressed and we are therefore not all that aware of it. We want the human body to smell of disinfectants rather than its own natural, interesting flavors. And so everybody is scrubbed and overcleaned and squirted with alcohol so that they won't smell, only they do smell—they smell like something from a lab and not like people.

One of the reasons that we find such difficulty being present to materiality is that we are afflicted with the strange notion that the material present is a hoax. Among other things, we have been told to not lay up treasure on the earth, where it will be corrupted by moths and rust, but to lay up treasure for ourselves in heaven. Actually, the treasure of heaven is now. We think that the real world is disintegrating and crumbling and therefore is bad, but the real reason we denigrate the world is because it is unseizable. It is always changing, we can't grasp it, and there's nothing to hold on to. But that's what makes it spiritual.

When you lean on the world, it collapses. So don't lean on it—live in it. Don't try to hold on to it. When you embrace someone, you don't squeeze the breath out of them and strangle them. You can't sense the world—you can't feel the world—if you grab hold of it. Use a light touch. Let it flow through your fingers. It's always slipping, so let it slip. And the more it runs, the more it stays, and the more it stays, the more it runs—that's the way it is. If you don't hold on to it, it's always here; if you do hold on to it, it's always running away. But if you use a light touch, you can discover the most shocking thing—the physical world right here and now, this absolutely concrete moment, is paradise. It's everything that you could ever have imagined the beatific vision to be.

When you read Dante's *Paradiso*, there is a fantastic description of rows of rainbows in which the center is a vivid white light that is so dazzling you can't look at it. From that center and moving out you see all of the colors of the spectrum, from violet all the way out to a transparent and luminous black, like obsidian. But then out beyond that it's white again, and you have a great arc of light, and the rays start waving and shimmering like waves and dancing in curlicues and engaging in every conceivable kind of complexity. Buddhist mandalas are like this, too, with radiances full of a myriad of Buddhas dancing, rattling bells, holding thunderbolts and swords, with more and more dimensions—color and smell and sound. And the sound gets so deep and bass and vibrant that it becomes solid and you can touch it.

That radiance and complexity are right here—they're never somewhere else. You don't get them anywhere but here. But if you try to find them and really pay attention and bring them into focus, you're just pushing them away. They have to come to you. You can't seek the present, because the moment you seek it you're not looking at the real present—you're looking at the one up ahead.

{ We live in a society in which we are more interested in accumulating the tokens of wealth than the actual wealth. }

What we call greed is essentially discontent with the present. Admittedly, there are too many people in the world living in poverty or on the edge of poverty who have an inadequate material present, but it is the greed of the well taken care of that is so terrifying. People who have enough to wear and eat are still greedy, and they are the ones who exploit the earth, drag every ounce of wealth out of it, generate all this rubbish and poisoned air, and all because they can't be here, alive in the present moment.

The pursuit of material pleasure is an art very much neglected in this day and age—an art that requires discipline, devotion, and skill. This art pertains to a broad array of activities and items already mentioned—cooking, clothing, furniture, lovemaking, child-rearing—as well as engineering, architecture, music, literature, painting, sculpture, and so forth. Unfortunately, we are living in a culture in which the pursuit of material pleasure is neglected in pursuit of symbolic pleasure.

A unit of money is useful in the same way that inches, hours, days, months, pounds, grams, and other units of measure are useful. Nobody goes around bragging about collecting grams or inches, because it is not a matter of social agreement that possessing grams or inches represents the possession of wealth. The only validity for money having any value whatsoever is that everybody agrees that particular denominations are worth so much, because dollars are exactly like poker chips, with the exception that all of us agree that we will accept dollars in lieu of goods and services. But it's those goods and services that constitute real wealth. It's just that we live in a society in which we are more interested in accumulating the tokens of wealth than the actual wealth—we'd rather eat the menu than the dinner. We see this in all dimensions of life, because we tend on the whole to confuse symbols with reality.

The idea that the world we perceive with our five senses is a material world is merely an idea. Materialism is a philosophy of nature—whether dialectical materialism or naturalistic materialism, it's just a point of view. It's merely a highly abstract notion. It's also purely conceptual to say that the world we perceive with our five senses is mental or spiritual because the actual world is neither. There's no way of saying what it is exactly. It's ineffable.

So the world that is neither spiritual nor material is the neglected world. Most people consider it as something material, but it's quite overlooked. And regardless, we have substituted symbols for whatever it is. We have symbolic goods, we live in symbolic homes, drive symbolic automobiles, and wear symbolic clothes—everything is valued for what it costs as opposed to its quality. As I've said elsewhere, nowhere is this more evident than in the food we eat, epitomized most by our bread. Bread is supposed to be our staff of life, but instead we consume a kind of Styrofoam that's fortified with vitamins, with a list of chemical ingredients on the back that we read as if it were medicine.

Neither do we truly enjoy the pursuit of pleasure in the form of the fine arts. An enormous number of people attend concerts and exhibitions of paintings simply because they think they're improving their minds by doing so, that they're doing something good for themselves in much the same way that most people attend church. That's an absolutely morbid interest. It also distracts you from what is actually going on. If you listen to Bach because you think it's good for you, you're not listening. In order to listen to Bach you have to swing with it, and then you forget all about whether it's good for you or not.

I don't like the distinction between lower and higher pleasures, but I will say that unless you have the realization that the pursuit of material pleasure requires a certain degree of asceticism, you will not be able to pursue any form of pleasure whatsoever. Asceticism is not unpleasant; asceticism is like the olive you have between wines to cleanse the palate. Furthermore, there's nothing wrong with olives.

People these days love the dreadful exercise known as jogging. There's absolutely nothing to recommend it. When I watch people jogging, they immediately show that they don't know how to run—they land on their heels in a way that jars their bones all the way up their vertebrae. They also move along with a certain grim determination in straight lines because that's supposed to be the shortest distance between two points, except it isn't, because the earth isn't a flat surface—it's wiggly.

The world is a fundamentally wiggly phenomenon, but wherever humans go we exert our passion for Euclideanism. We put everything in boxes and rule things out in straight lines like the grid patterns of our streets we impose upon the surface of the earth. Whenever you see straight lines like that, you know that humans have been there. But why all this passion for Euclidean order? Mr. Euclid had an extremely simple mind that tended to think in rather uninteresting shapes instead of curvaceous wiggles. Wiggliness offends some people. They're not quite sure of it, they can't figure it out, and they never quite know what it's going to do next. That's why people don't like snakes. Snakes are wonderful symbols of wiggly vitality, of undulation and waves. All the world is fundamentally a system of vibrating waves.

If you can't wave with it—if you are rigid—you will always be resisting life. Going with wiggliness and swinging with it is fundamental to the pleasures of life, which is why we call those who cannot do so "straights" and "squares." They do not swing. Instead, they're always trying to square things away and get things straight. As a result, they are out of harmony with the wiggly universe.

Most religions are square, too. They resist the flow element in life. They want canals instead of rivers and conceive of heaven as a city instead of a garden. After all, paradise was a garden, and that's where all the trouble began. So people substituted the heavenly city for the paradise garden, and popes began to call themselves "Urban." Unbelievers were called "pagans" because a *pagano* was a rustic person who lived in the country, and people who live in the country understand wiggles. They are distinct from people of the streets. They live under the sky as opposed to inside a box.

Wiggles, Seriousness, and the Fear of Pleasure

The box is our great symbol of classification. What box are you in? All words are boxes: animal, vegetable, mineral, solid, gas, liquid, Republican, Democrat, capitalist, communist, Christian, heathen, male, female, and so on. All boxes. And because we think in boxes, we live in boxes—poorly made, identical boxes. Instead, consider the types of fish who make homes in beautiful shells with glorious spirally wiggles on them and lovely colors. But we want everything straightened out, and that rigidity is always in contrast with the fluidity that surrounds us. We are landlubbers, as opposed to people of the waves, although we Brits have always made a great deal of associating freedom with the ocean.

{ The art of faith is not in taking a stand but in learning how to swim. }

We think of the sea as fluid and the land as solid, but nothing could be further from the truth. Where I live, in Sausalito, a lot of land was reclaimed along the waterfront, and they dredged out mud to make the marina, not realizing that land, too, is liquid. So the land adjoining the water is sinking because it's filling up the hole made by the excavation. People don't think of things like this, because they conceive of land as purely solid.

Even in religion we are seemingly looking for solids, for somewhere we can take our stand—a firm foundation, the rock of ages, even Paul Tillich's "ground of being." But that's not the sort of universe we live in. Our universe is fluid, and so the art of faith is not in taking a stand but in learning how to swim. You don't cling to water; you don't try to stand on it. You breathe, relax, and learn to trust that the water will support you. This is also true for flying, gliding, and sailing—all of these arts have adapted to the fluid. And that's what we must learn if we want to survive as a species and survive happily. Instead, we cling to what we think is solid. Even more, we demand more and more solidity. Nothing ruins pleasure more than the anxiety to go on having it—more, more, and more. That just shows that you aren't having it now; you always think it's something that's on its way. You'd rather have jam tomorrow than jam today. When we think that something is useless, we say it has no *future*, and that's the most awful thing you could say about something. It would be better to say that it has no *present*. A future is just a promise, just as we write checks as a promise to pay. Promises, promises . . .

Learning to wiggle is fundamental to pleasure. We should let go and relax. But that doesn't mean that we become droopy—relaxing means becoming supple. It means learning your weight, how to use it, and how to flow with gravity. Water always takes the course of least resistance—it flows and wiggles with gravity—and yet it possesses tremendous strength. For most of us, especially white Anglo-Saxon Protestants and Irish Catholics, taking the path of least resistance is somehow considered cowardly and despicable. You've got to get there the fastest way possible, which is again in a straight line, the supposed shortest distance between two points.

That's why jogging isn't the right way to run. The right way to run is by dancing. You should dance across the countryside, and anyone who does so will outwit and out-time the jogger. I watched the Brazilian team win the World Cup in soccer, and I've never seen anything like it—it certainly isn't how they taught us to play soccer in school. As one of the sportswriters at the London *Times* put it, the Brazilians danced their way to victory. It was like watching the most beautiful form of basketball—instead of this tough, pushing form of ball control, they engaged in the most incredible teamwork with subtle passing and bounced the ball off every part of their bodies—backs, shoulders, hips, heads, everything. It was a beautiful and magnificent spectacle.

We are not taught to do things like that. We are taught that life is serious, and therefore life must be done in an efficient way. In ancient times, people sang while they worked, but hardly anybody sings anymore unless it's part of an official performance. Imagine a bank teller singing as they counted out your money. If that happened, you'd probably complain to management. "This money is quite serious—no one should be singing about it!" Can you imagine a stockbroker's work song? I once had my shoes shined in a New York subway, and the man who did it sang and gave the most extraordinary performance. He was swinging.

When most people drive a bus through city traffic, they're fighting the clock, cursing and sweating, and they're often quite angry. Imagine instead that driving a bus wasn't about getting from here to there but just about going. You could just dance that bus through the streets, dodge traffic skillfully and gracefully, and when you did stop at a light or get into a jam, you'd just play a little tune on the horn, pass jokes to the cab driver next to you, play with the passengers, and so on.

People don't usually perform their jobs that way because work is supposed to be serious business—not pleasant at all. You get paid for it, after all, and you're not supposed to get paid for enjoying yourself. For the West, the curse of work arose in the story of Genesis. The tree of knowledge wasn't about the knowledge of good and evil in the ordinary sense but about the knowledge of what is advantageous and disadvantageous. What's advantageous in life when it comes to work is swinging it.

That's what I try to do. I think I'm smart, I talk and write about all of these things, but I don't do so because I think I'm doing you any good—I just do so because I like it. And if I get paid for it, then it's how I make my living. It's as simple as that. I'm just a philosophical entertainer.

In fact, I've been trying for a long time to sell the idea of a television show called *Delight from Asia*, but so far I've had no takers. It's meant to expose Westerners to some of the pleasurable refinements of the various cultures of Asia and at the same time gently twit the American public for not really knowing how to spend their money.

One of the most curious things about Westerners is our fear of pleasure and our incapacity for indulging in it as a consequence of this fear. I constantly marvel that the richest nation on earth—money-wise, that is—takes such dreary pleasures when it could afford much more elaborate ones. It's said that the French eat with gusto and the British eat apologetically. I guess it's because we believe we shouldn't enjoy or think too much about what we're eating, whereas French people love to celebrate and talk about food. There's something slightly vulgar about that to us—eating is, after all, a bit animalistic. We consider it highly impolite to smack our lips and burp, whereas other cultures do so naturally as a sign of appreciation.

Most Westerners eat out of duty. We eat only because it is nutritious—it's good for us. As Henry Miller writes, we "throw something down the hatch" and swallow a dozen vitamins.[1] There are probably various complex reasons for our odd reluctance to enjoy life with gusto, but one of them is the fact that we believe that God may be watching. There's a feeling that we're not supposed to get too involved in pleasure, and if we enjoy ourselves thoroughly and become too boisterous, then someone's going to punish us. Or maybe it's because we're afraid that pleasure will in some way suck us in and beguile us, turning us into helpless addicts to something or the other.

That explains why we're so standoffish about the whole thing. Of course, there's some sense to this attitude. It was once quite difficult to feed and clothe the vast majority of human beings. We lived in an age of scarcity, which made it understandably wicked to waste any food or materials whatsoever. When I first moved to the United States, my mother came to visit us and was appalled at the fact that my wife poured some milk down the drain—she wanted us to put it to use in some way, to make a custard out of it or something. That's how the world was, but today—at least for most of us living in the United States—we're living in an economy of waste.

The fact of the matter is that we are moving into a period of economic development in which it is genuinely possible to adequately feed and clothe every human being on the planet. All that the sovereign nations of the world have spent on waging war in the past century could have gone instead toward supplying everybody on earth with a decent, independent income. But, you see, politicians and businesspeople are not practical. They might say they're hardheaded and realistic, but as a matter of fact they're just shortsighted and only look to attain immediate objectives. They're incapable of comparing the costs.

The Failure of Money and Technology

If it weren't for the failure of one of our networks—the information network of money—we could apply our technology to feeding the world properly. We have

the most unbelievable superstitions and psychological blocks about money, which Freud equates with our
attitudes about excrement. Whatever the cause may
be, it's a major obstacle to developing our technology
properly and enabling it to do what it is supposed to
do, which is to save labor, produce goods and services,
and so on.

{ *In the end, money is nothing
but bookkeeping.* }

I want to insert a story here, one that is entirely
legendary and apocryphal. At some point in time, the
great banks of the world became absolutely sick of the
expense and security measures involved in shipping
consignments of gold from one bank to another. So
they decided that all of them would open offices on
a certain island in the South Pacific—a balmy and
comfortable island—and there they would store all
of the gold in the entire world. They placed the gold
in enormous subterranean vaults that could only be
reached by deep elevator shafts. All the gold was in one
place, and the chief banks could easily keep track of it
and make transactions there among themselves.

This was all very efficient. It went on beautifully for
several years. Eventually, the presidents of these banks
decided to have a convention on the island and bring their
wives and families and so on. They did so, inspected the

books while they were there—everything was beautifully in order—and a number of their children really wanted to see all of that gold. So the presidents asked the managers to take them down into the vaults with their children so that the children could see the gold.

"Well," the managers said, "that's a bit inconvenient at this time, and we don't think the children would be that interested anyway. After all, it's just plain old gold."

But the presidents insisted. "No, no. Come now. The kids will be thrilled. Let's go down and see that gold." And then there was further hemming and hawing and delays of one sort or the other, but the presidents eventually won out.

But they never got to see the gold because the managers finally revealed that a few years prior there had been a catastrophic earthquake—all the vaults had been swallowed up, and the gold had disappeared somewhere down there in the earth. Other than that, everything had been going just fine. The bookkeeping had been kept in perfect order all along.

In the end, money is nothing but bookkeeping. It's just numbers. Money is a way of measuring what you owe the community or what the community owes you. It was intended as an improvement on barter. At one time, if you worked on a farm, the farmer paid you in ears of corn, heads of cabbage, onions, and other vegetables. If you wanted something like a pot or pan, you took some of your vegetables to whomever made pots and pans and made an exchange. But someone decided it was too inconvenient to carry around all these loads of goods, so they began to use cowry shells, which eventually became gold, and gold was used because it was reportedly rare and therefore able to maintain constant value. As the economy of the Western world developed, it turned out there wasn't enough gold to go around, and instead of simply dropping the prices of goods and services to keep pace with the amount of gold in circulation, we developed a system of credit, which is simply bookkeeping.

Eventually, this led to all of the great industrial nations of the world finding themselves heavily in debt. Our national debt—much to the horror and consternation of old-fashioned Republicans—grows bigger by the year. And the reason it grows bigger by the year is that with an expanding gross national product, you need more and more money in order to circulate the amount of goods produced, which is also ever increasing.

Now, I'm not an economist, but any fool can see there's something amiss here. I've studied the work of Robert Theobald, who is a futurist and economist who asserts that money in itself has no value—it's just a circulation of information.[2] Gold might be said to have value because it can be used in dentistry and jewelry, but as a means of exchanging goods and services it's as primitive as using horses to carry the mail. Money is a pure abstraction. The trouble with most people is that they still think money is real, but it isn't. Money has the same relationship to real wealth as words have to the physical world. Words are not the same thing as the physical world, and money is simply an accounting of available energy—economic energy.

Introducing technology into production yields enormous quantities of goods. At the same time, it puts people out of work. Now, you can argue that technology also creates jobs, but most of them will be futile endeavors involved with making all kinds of frippery and unnecessary contraptions. To make this all work, someone has to beguile the public into feeling that they need and want these completely gratuitous objects that aren't even beautiful to begin with. And to keep everyone working, we have to create an excessive amount of nonsense employment and busywork—bureaucratic and otherwise—because we believe it simply must be so. In particular, as good Protestants we believe that work prevents the devil from making work for idle hands.

We've completely overlooked some basic principles. Machines were supposed to make drudgery unnecessary. Unfortunately, we haven't allowed technology to achieve its purpose, so we live in a constant state of self-frustration. If a manufacturer automates a plant and therefore dismisses the labor force, the workers no longer have the income to buy those products, which means that the investment in expensive automative machinery served no purpose. Obviously, the public has to be provided with the means of purchasing what machines produce, and the answer to that problem comes back to the machines. The machine works for the manufacturer and for the community, which isn't to put forward a statist, communist idea of expropriation but only to say that the government—and its people—have to be responsible for issuing to themselves sufficient credit to circulate the goods they produce and that they themselves have to balance the measuring standard of money with the gross national product.

Theobald says that everyone should be assured of a minimum income. This idea horrifies most people—they'll go on and on about wasteful, lazy people. But just look at what happened during the Great Depression, when in the middle of plenty and abundance a very rich country became broke and miserable and starving all due to this psychological hang-up, which is that money is real and people are supposed to suffer in order to obtain it.

But the whole point of the machine was to relieve us of this suffering. As far as technology goes, we're living in the current times, but psychologically we're still back in the seventeenth century. And our hang-ups about money and wealth and pleasure and the nature of work are all formidable problems.

The Problem of Guilt

It will take the best brains in public relations and propaganda across all sorts of media to get across the message to the general public about what money actually is. Otherwise, we'll remain stuck in this inflationary cycle in which more paper money is produced and the prices keep rising higher and higher, which is stupid. Unfortunately, the least effective way of persuading people is to pass laws, but we must find some way to persuade people not to raise prices, to play fair, and to keep some sort of standard correspondence between how much is produced and how much credit is issued. And this is a deep issue for us because it comes down to a problem we have about guilt.

The difference between having a job and having a vocation is that a job is something unpleasant you do in order to make money. There are plenty of jobs out there because there will always be a certain amount of dirty work that nobody wants to do, and they are therefore willing to pay someone else to do it for them. But that type of work is also diminishing due to technology and mechanization. If you take a job for the sole purpose of making money, you are absurd. When money becomes the goal, you inevitably will confuse it with happiness and pleasure.

We have inherited an ancient guilt that says if we don't work, then we have no right to eat. There are people out there in the world who don't have enough to eat, so we shouldn't really enjoy our dinner, even though we have no possible means of conveying food to them. And the thing about guilt is that it's a foolproof way of not doing anything about a situation. When people feel guilty, they don't seek out practical solutions but instead resort to all sorts of symbolic methods of expiation—they go to confession, they visit psychotherapists, and so on. They do all sorts of things that have nothing to do with the problem itself and everything to do with feeling okay about it. Guilt is a destructive emotion. We need to take a different attitude toward our mistakes and misdeeds.

In *Leaves of Grass*, Walt Whitman writes that he admires animals because "they do not lie awake in the dark and weep for their sins." Animals are practical, as are children who have yet to be taught this extraordinary hang-up of guilt. When most adults do something wrong or make a mistake, someone else makes us feel guilty and ashamed of it, so as a consequence we run around licking the sores of our wounded ego about it. What sense does this make? The first thing to understand is that making mistakes is natural. It's not a serious failing as a human being to do so. Everybody makes mistakes, and there's no way out of that. In fact, you can't learn anything unless you make mistakes.

{ *Freedom means being able to make mistakes; it means having the freedom to be a damn fool.* }

When I was first taught how to play the piano, I learned from a schoolmarm who placed an India rubber—they're called an eraser in the States—on top of each hand to help me maintain good posture. And every time I'd play a wrong note, she'd hit my fingers with a pencil. I knew an anthropologist who learned piano in the same manner, and as a result he grew up completely incapable of reading notes. But I had another piano teacher who taught me quite differently. She said, "You must not be afraid of playing the wrong notes. Just forget it. Play it wrong, go over it again, and you'll eventually get it right. Just keep the same rhythm going, even if you have to slow down. That way, even if it's the wrong note, it will still be the right rhythm."

This is how to work with people's blockages and guilt and shame about making mistakes. Freedom means being able to make mistakes; it means having the freedom to be a damn fool. Additionally, it means not recriminating yourself for mistakes but working to do something different in the future.

Catholics are renowned for their guilt, but on the whole they're a lot less guilty than Protestants. When the Protestants in England abandoned the auricular confession to a priest, they inserted a general confession in the prayer book that the congregation all says together. When Catholics make a confession to a priest, they do so by acknowledging the sin and calling upon John the Baptist, the holy apostles and saints, the Blessed Mary, and so on, and the priest then says something like "May the Almighty God have mercy upon you and forgive you your sins and bring you to everlasting life by the authority of our Lord Jesus Christ committed unto me, and I absolve thee from all sins in the name of the Father, the Son, and the Holy Spirit."

The Anglican formulary, however, takes this quite simple confession of sins before the whole company of heaven and turns it into an absolute grovel. You're supposed to say that you have sinned so horribly that the very remembrance of the sins is grievous and that the burden of them is intolerable. Thereafter follows cringing, crying, breast beating, and wallowing in guilt. In turn, the priest quotes all kinds of scriptural texts from the Bible to prove that those who earnestly repent will be forgiven by God, but the appeal to authority reveals a fundamental uncertainty here.

After Catholics confess their specific sins, they say something like "For these and all my sins, I firmly propose amendment and humbly ask pardon of God." This is where we find a fly in the ointment, because no sensitive Catholic can say—without having grave doubts about it—that they aren't going to do some of the offending things again. If you're a workaday Catholic, confession is a safety valve. You're going to go on living just as lackadaisically as ever, and you simply go to church and to confession every so often to get rid of the guilt and evil, sort of like going to the bathroom. That works as long as you don't get too thoughtful about whether or not you really mean what you say during confession.

Regardless of the type, most Christians carry around this idea that God keeps a black book somewhere in which he writes down every mistake you make. And when the day of judgment comes, there's going to be an accounting—the gatekeepers tally up all the good and evil you've done and weigh them on St. Michael's balance, just like in the *Egyptian Book of the Dead*. As a result of this belief, an enormously complicated system of celestial bookkeeping arose in the later part of the Middle Ages that had to do with the dispensation of surplus merits and indulgences. And if you said certain prayers or committed yourself to certain pilgrimages or—most importantly—made monetary contributions, you would receive plenary or partial indulgences against your time in purgatory. In this way, people used an enormously complicated banking system to settle their heavenly accounts by using credit issued by saints who were themselves producing a surplus of goods—just like machines.

4

In Praise of
Swinging

The first principle in the art of pleasure is swinging, which simply means that you mustn't take anything seriously. Life is a form of dancing, and dancing isn't serious—that's why it's prohibited by fundamentalists of all types and other gloomy sorts. They don't approve of dancing. It isn't because dancing is sexy—you can dance with anyone or all by yourself—it's because dancing is considered frivolous and undignified. But what is the virtue in being stiff and rigid? As Lao Tzu said, when people are born they are supple and tender; when they die they are stiff and hard. Plants are like this as well—the young ones are juicy and soft, and the old ones are brittle and dry. Suppleness and softness are clearly signs of life.

Rigidity and Identity

I suppose that some men confuse psychic rigidity with having an erection. They substitute guns, rockets, and vehicles to manifest a type of masculinity that isn't there. The real secret to women's liberation is their wiggliness—they are gentle, but with the power of water. To quote Lao Tzu from the *Tao Te Ching* again, "The valley spirit does not die." The spirit of the valley was supposed to be feminine, whereas the mountains were said to be male. If a man wants to be a universal channel, he should have a certain feminine element about him—something playful, lilting, curvaceous, soft, and all of that which is so neglected by Euclideans. It's the principle of life and of nature. Being rigid and resistant to change—resistant to life—is almost useless.

But it's just that sense of rigidity—of muscular tension—that underlies the physical basis of our sense of identity. We can illustrate this by comparing the processes of seeing and watching. When we're simply receiving visual input from the phenomenal world, our eyes are at rest while they take in all this play of light and color, but when we're watching something—that is, looking hard at it and trying to pay attention with our eyes—the muscles around our eyes tense up, our face tightens, and we expend far more energy than is necessary. To adjust our vision, the focal muscles of our eyes need only to open or close a small aperture. That's it. It doesn't take much effort at all to do that.

In fact, the effort we make when we look hard at something distracts our eyes from seeing accurately, but we feel as if we must constantly make an effort in everything we do. All of this absurd muscular straining and gritting of teeth doesn't help anything other than to further promote the illusion of a separate thing we call *I*. That sensation of totally unnecessary strain that exists all the time is the ego—a physical referent of the idea of ego. And it's that gratuitous strain that tells us we exist. Our psychic staring is the ego we feel at the center of ourselves, and that stands in opposition and resistance to all I define as not myself. That rigidity of holding off life so that I can maintain my particular shape, form, and place is what makes us uptight and unable to swing through the fear of what might happen if we'd only let things wiggle.

{ *If you don't go crazy at regular intervals, you'll eventually go insane.* }

A nonwiggly person is unadaptive in a wiggly world, and so we develop these insect-like, mechanical behavioral patterns that have to go on and on with regularity, always the same—chug, chug, chug—but they're not adaptable. They don't hold up, and we can see it happening all around us; the pavement is cracking, and the grass is growing through. I recently heard somebody say that we're eventually going to be left with nothing but crows, crabgrass, and inedible fish. So we need to do something. Not by preaching at people and condemning them—which, once again, simply doesn't work—but by wooing them. In that way, maybe we can all come off it.

Sunday was supposed to be the day to swing. The Bible says that God worked for six days, and on the seventh day he rested. It was a time-out—a time-out from being rational and methodical and efficient. Instead, on Sunday we go to church, and the preacher says blah, blah, blah, and he lays down the law, law, law. In other words, he throws the book at us. He wears the same robe as a judge, and not only does he tell us what to do, he also tells God what to do. It's endless talk. Occasionally there are songs, but the hymns are just religious nursery rhymes with dreadful tunes and stupid words, and nobody dances, and there's nothing mysterious or magical at all that happens, except perhaps in the Catholic Church, and even they are trying to get rid of all of that.

If we don't take a break from time to time, we're going to collapse. That's what Sundays and Mardi Gras and carnivals and the original orgies (which were secret rites in the worship of Dionysus or Bacchus) were for. You've got to let loose and swing and go crazy every now and then, because if you don't go crazy at regular intervals, you'll eventually go insane.

I should add that it won't do to make another project out of all of this. It would be easy for us to become rigid about derigidifying ourselves. People pursue all sorts of psychotherapy, exercise, sensory awareness training, encounter groups, yoga, and so on to loosen up, but they try to do so in such a grim mood. There's actually a book out there entitled *You Must Relax*. It's the same thing with people who retire and think they're going to have fun and enjoy their lives, so maybe they get up in the morning so they can hit the golf course early, but instead of enjoying golf—which is entirely possible—they begin to measure their game in terms of athletics or mathematics. What's my score? How much have I improved? They adopt the religion of golf and play all sorts of social games that are tied up with it, and it's a very serious matter. And when golf is over, they head over to the bridge table and do the same. Eventually, when they're completely worn out, they'll get vaguely drunk, and the grim pursuit of pleasure goes on and on.

It's the same thing with religious people. They do their daily meditations—say, forty minutes every morning before breakfast. There are all of these steps and stages to go through. And they spend their time wondering which teachers are best and which teachers are phony. Maybe Swami so-and-so is not quite the real thing because real swamis can perform magic and remain undecomposed after death for an indefinite period of time without the benefit of embalming. See? It's the same old thing. The same temperament that wants to control and manage the so-called material world will do the very same thing when it comes to the so-called spiritual world. People want the most efficient yoga because they want to get there fast—they want to get there now.

Where is it that they want to get? What do you want? Where are you going? Few people know. Some people do have a precise or disciplined sense of what they want, and when they get it, they stop, but there are very few people like that. When most people think of pleasure, they don't have a very definite idea of what it is, and if they do have a definite idea of pleasure, it turns out when they get it that it isn't what they actually wanted. So where are you going? And what's the rush?

Look around. Pay attention. You may already be there—it's just that you didn't notice. From the point of view of someone who's starving in a Calcutta slum, all of us are as fortunate as maharajas. Even the most penurious person among us is, by comparison, a maharaja. So maybe you're already there. You've already arrived.

Here's where somebody will say, "No, no, no—you see, it can't last. Eventually I'm going to die and just be a corpse," and that gives them the horrors. And maybe their death will be a slow disintegration, a painful route to the end involving a hospital and a lot of tubes. And in their fear and desire to overcome that, they turn to religion. They acknowledge that physical demise is an unfortunate limitation of the body, so they begin to identify themselves as something beyond the body—the true vehicle of their personality that will go on and on. That way, they won't lose everything they've acquired. They can smuggle something across the border. Maybe the guards won't notice because the baggage is spiritual.

We've heard of the pearly gates that are supposed to serve as the entryway to heaven. People usually think of these as gates that are decorated with pearls, but the gate of heaven is actually just one pearl with a small hole with a piece of string through it. And you've got to travel through that hole to get in, and you obviously can't do that with a lot of baggage—you have to leave your past behind you.

Now Is When the World Begins

What happens to you when you get rid of your past? What happens when you forget it all, including who you are? What remains? Not your education, nor your ancestry, nor any of your distinguished accomplishments. All of that is in the past, which—after all—doesn't exist. Where is it? Turn your common sense around and see that your past isn't pushing you forward into the equally imaginable future. You're simply leaving it behind, like tracks. It isn't pushing you anywhere unless you insist that it is.

You can always pass the buck. People love to do that. Maybe you think you're a neurotic mess because your mother was a neurotic mess, and so you were never given a fair chance in life. And your mother might say that she couldn't help it because she herself had an appalling father and a dreadful mother, and if you were to ask them, they would point back to their own equally neurotic parents. Everybody is looking back over their shoulder and passing the buck—all the way back to Adam and Eve, and we know what happened there. They passed the buck to the serpent. And when God looked at the serpent, the serpent didn't say anything, because the serpent doesn't have a past—it's a wiggle. The serpent wiggles from its head all the way down to its tail.

Are you a head or are you a tail? Do you move backward or forward? Which way are you going? If you truly leave your past behind you, it can no longer drive you. It just wells up out of a mysterious present, always new. This very moment is the creation of the universe. Now.

If you look back and back in time and wonder about the origin of the big bang, all you'll see are vanishing traces. The big bang is happening now. Now is when the world begins.

People think, instead, that the big bang was something that happened billions of years ago—that at some point everything inexplicably blew up out of nothingness and that the galaxies expanded from an infinitely small center and are still moving outward into the future. And maybe the whole thing will come back together again someday and then blow up once more. Who knows? Maybe everything will fade out, but then it will be back to where it was again before it all started. What happened once can always happen again. Pulsation is the very nature of life—big pulses and tiny pulses, pulses within pulses, forever and ever.

But it's you who is doing all of this, only you're not doing it by straining. A *you* deeper than the straining you is doing all of this. It's the same *you* that grows your hair and colors your eyes and designs your thumbprints and all of this—all without thinking, all without straining. That's the you that creates the world, right now.

Instead of thinking of the past as the reality that explains everything that's happening right now, let's look at now and see it happening. Where does now happen from? That's a question only asked by people who think that the past causes the present—they always want to know where it comes from. Who started it? What made it happen? But what if nothing made it happen—what if it just happens?

All of these questions—Where is it? What is reality? What is now? What is life? What is it that you want?—can't be answered by a type of analysis that breaks things down into their components. And you won't find the answers by labeling things in various ways, classifying, putting things in boxes, tidying up, and so on. That's how we tidy up—we throw things in a box. Boxes inside boxes inside boxes. But when it's all boxed up, you can't see it anymore, so instead of putting it in boxes, let's just look at it the way it comes. You can only find out what it is by looking at it and feeling it directly.

Are We Going to Make It?

From the point of view of cosmic consciousness, the good and evil things that human beings do are in a type of balance, just as the varied behavior of other creatures—insects, worms, fish, and flowers—is in balance. As Chuang Tzu said, only knaves and fools believe you can have the positive without the negative, the yang without the yin.

> { Part of the joy of life comes from the
> process of trying to get rid of evil. }

This is hard for Westerners to accept, especially Christians, because we're dedicated to the abolition of evil. I think Jews are much more sensible about this, because they don't view evil as something extraneous to God. As it says in Isaiah 45, "I am the Lord, and there is none else. I form the light, and create darkness. I make peace, and create evil. I the Lord do all these things." The Jews believe that at the beginning of creation, God implanted in the human heart something called the *yetzer hara*—the wayward spirit inclined to violate the will of God. And if God hadn't done so, human life would be insipid and without the least significance. So God is responsible for evil because he placed it in people to give them something to fight against.

On one level, the evil side of things is part of the total harmony. Its function is to give you something to chew on, to work at. You'll never get rid of it, but part of the joy of life comes from the process of trying to get rid of evil. The function of the devil is to always be losing the battle, but the battle is never fully lost; the function of the good side, on the other hand, is to always be winning the battle but to never fully emerge as the final victor.

Of course, we can solve certain problems in the world—for example, we can establish a world in which people aren't committed to drudgery—but we'll simply discover social evil in some new form. It's the same thing as when you're worried sick about money, you don't know how you're going to make the payments on the house and the car and the insurance and all of that, and you suddenly come into the money you need. For a couple of days, you're ecstatic—you're walking on air. Before you know it, you start thinking about what could go wrong. You could get sick, the government might cause you problems, or burglars might break into your house and steal everything. And you start worrying about all of that with the same intensity as you did earlier when you were so concerned about not having enough money to pay the bills. If you're a worry bird, you'll always find something to worry about.

This is because we're always in the same place. This is one understanding of relativity. When I was a child, British dentistry was abominable—it was simply torture—so I am thankful indeed for American dentistry. I experienced that contrast, so I'm in a position to appreciate relativity as it applies to dental care. My children, on the other hand, have only known American dentistry, so they are less appreciative of the situation and have, therefore, other worries.

As Meister Eckhart said, if a stone were as aware as an angel, a stone could be as happy as an angel—or perhaps as miserable. The problem of life—at every level of evolution—is always the same. The pressing question remains: Are we going to make it?

The Hindus teach that God is playing hide-and-seek with himself, that Brahman—the supreme self—deliberately falls into the illusion of Maya and pretends that he's one of us. Each time, God thinks up some fantastic way of getting lost and goes far out enough to forget that he's playing a game in the first place. Each one of us is one of those ways of getting lost and forgetting the game. And all of these horrors and appalling situations that we experience lead us to ask, "Am I gonna make it?" And the answer often seems to be no. We might get away with it for a little while, but in the end we aren't going to make it.

But why not? Well, look at a star. A star lasts for what seems like a long time as a great burst of fire, and the fire gets bigger and bigger and hotter and hotter until it eventually begins to diminish and fade. At some point, the energy falls away, and there's darkness. Every star does this. At some point, the light has to give up, because if the radiance never gave up—if it just continued to grow until it filled everything—there would be no way for it to realize itself. Because you can only realize light by the contrast of darkness.

If you are a ray emanating from the Godhead, what does it matter if you're long or short? People want to live to be ninety or a hundred, as if that's a measure of success. Everybody wants to be a long ray. There's a Zen teaching from Ryokan that says, "In the scenery of spring, there is nothing superior, nothing inferior. Flowering branches grow naturally—some short, some long."[1] If you look at a star or some sort of stellar object, it's only interesting if its rays are of unequal length. If the rays were all equal, it would appear flat and mechanical and quite unlike gorgeous radiolaria or the minute animalcules of the ocean. Overall, they might have a globular form, but when you examine them closely, their stems are all of different lengths.

Are we going to make it? That is always the question. From one way of looking at it, we're certainly not going to make it—the ray fizzles out, and we call that death. But that's only true if you think that you're the ray.

You aren't the ray as much as you are the source of the ray, and the source doesn't vanish or fizzle out. The source is always there, shooting out rays and letting them vanish. At every stage of the universe—whether you are up there with the gods or down here with the human refuse—you are basically in the same situation. Everybody is essentially the divine being working out the panorama of life in a myriad of ways, and these different ways require spectra of all kinds—the spectrum of color, the spectrum of tones, and the spectrum of being.

In one version of the color spectrum, one end is purple and the other is red, but when you really examine what constitutes purple, you'll find red in there because the spectrum goes all the way around. Spectra shouldn't be laid out and represented as something that is stretched out from left to right on a horizontal tape—a circular interpretation communicates something that no amount of words could convey. It speaks to our unconscious, to depths of understanding far more subtle than our intellectual thinking can grasp. And maybe in the center of a circular version of the color spectrum you'd find white light that is neither good nor bad, neither up nor down—it's just what there is. Suchness. As the Chinese say, the true center of a circle is any point on the circumference because that's where you can begin or end the circle at any point.

There's a Zen koan that says, "Indra built a seamless tower." Without the seam, there's no way of telling where it begins and ends. Similarly, in nature we find a seamless order in which every point is central and therefore feels similar to all other points, which is to say that the beings there envy those who appear above and pity those below. Who knows—maybe the most primitive animalcules imaginable have pity on the angels.

Polarization and Contrast

The human being is designed to perceive everything by contrast. There's no way of knowing whether the real world is arranged by contrast, but we are essentially systems composed of neurons in an extraordinarily complicated pattern based on a simple principle called "Is You Is, or Is You Ain't?" That's the fundamental contrast.

Neurons either fire or they don't. You could represent this in the same binary arithmetic used in digital computers—a firing neuron by the number 1, a non-firing neuron by 0. Out of these two integers you can represent all conceivable numbers, and messages in this language can convey all sorts of information—mathematical, verbal, but also visual (for example, the colors that come out of a television). With the same notation, we can convey solid objects at one end of a process and have them come out at the other end engraved in plastic, enlarged, or diminished by lasers or other forms of technology. And so it's tempting to say that the principle of "Is You Is, or Is You Ain't?" is fundamental to the entire universe.

This is what the Taoists believed. Yin and yang are the negative and positive principles, and in the *I Ching* you'll see various combinations of these that constitute the sixty-four basic situations of life. A hexagram is made up of six lines, and the Chinese took hexagrams and represented yang with an unbroken line and yin with a broken one. This means that you have six lines with two possibilities for each: therefore, sixty-four different hexagrams. And when it came time to make a decision, they would by a random process arrive at one of these hexagrams and then use that to make their decision. It's like tossing a coin, but a coin with sixty-four sides to it. Heads or tails, yang or yin.

When we apply this principle to the pursuit of pleasure, we come to realize that we cannot have pleasure without the contrast with nonpleasure. If we want one, we must have the other. You can't have a one-ended spectrum any more than you could have a magnet with just one pole. Recognizing this fact seems to put an awful kibosh on everything we're trying to do—everything we want to achieve, every sort of progress we're after—and that's dispiriting, to say the least. But let's look into this business a bit more thoroughly.

If all I can see before me is a black background, there's nothing particular to register my attention—I'm as good as blind. Similarly, if I'm confronted with a purely white background, there's nothing particular there to attract my attention—I also might as well be blind. However, if I'm a naughty little boy and I place a mark on a black wall with my piece of chalk or take some charcoal to a spotless white wall, I have some contrast—and, in these examples, a relationship between positive and negative. Which is which? It doesn't matter. I can call white negative and black positive or vice versa, but it's difficult to do both at the same time.

That being said, the two are as different as different can be. Most of the time we use the word *polarization* rather incorrectly to indicate an increase in societal discord, but polarization is actually a form of harmony. The two poles of the earth are the harmony of the earth. The two poles of a magnet are the harmony of the magnet—they are polarized, and yet they have common ground. In the case of the earth, it's the earth itself that's common ground between the North and South Poles. In this way, black and white—positive and negative—are as different as different can be, but they're also the same. They are different aspects of the same field.

This brings us to the difference between exoteric and esoteric points of view in philosophy, religion, and so on. The exoteric point of view emphasizes black and white with respect to their differences—good and bad, life and death, light and darkness, and so on. It's the exoteric point of view that presents God as light—a light in which there is no darkness. But within every religion there's a secret, and that's the esoteric thing. That's only something that's revealed to initiates, to people who can stand it. And the esoteric view is simply that black and white, although explicitly different, are implicitly one.

You can't have one without the other. You could even say that black *is* white and white *is* black, if by the word *is* you mean "implies." As the Buddhists say, emptiness is form and form is emptiness. The Chinese have a particular way of saying it that doesn't translate very well into English—it's more like *void that form and form that void,* but what that really means is something like "implies" or "goes with."

We don't let out the esoteric message in church. We don't say that God has a dark side as well, even though it says so in Isaiah 45. Even so, we're afraid to let that out because we think that maybe there's somebody out there who will justify murder by saying it's necessary in order for you to know how nice people can be, or maybe that you need somebody to steal from you or cheat you in order for you to recognize goodness and honesty, just in the same way that you need the occasional rain to truly appreciate the sunshine. St. Paul wrestled with this very problem. He wondered if the law of Moses was what had made people conscious of right and wrong and if sin might actually be necessary in order for grace to abound.

The esoteric thing is what you keep out of the hands of children, just as it says on a bottle of poison: "Keep away from children." And yet we have uses for poison—it's dangerous but necessary for some things, so there's a balancing act. The way we balance our uses for evil usually involves establishing an in-group and forbidding violence against any of its members, but it's okay to commit evil against outsiders. This is how the Jews and blacks have been persecuted for the longest time—they're defined as outsiders, as not actually human. In the same way, we can label someone insane and deprive them of their civil rights without due process. They're just bodies without working minds—as we say, they're not "all there." It's the same with heretics, lepers, and other outcasts. When we define someone as less than human, they are denied all protections granted to the in-group.

We find these dynamics at play as well in the distinction between self and other. That which I consider myself and that which I exclude from that category are not in the same type of contrasting relationship as the two ends of a pole. It's more like the center and circumference of a circle, with me in the middle and you on the periphery—one end is still, and the other end is moving. Unless I have a sympathetic relationship with you, I do not know your thoughts, and I do not feel your pleasures or pains. I consider my actions voluntary and yours involuntary—at least they're involuntary as far as I'm concerned.

Of course, I wouldn't be able to realize what I call my *self* without contrasting it to others. *Self* only means *self* because *other* means *other*, just as *is* only means *is* because of *isn't*. Just like black and white, there's a mutual relationship between them. This implies that self and other go together, and so they are inseparable.

This brings us again to the distinction between what we consider voluntary and what we call involuntary, that is, what we do and what happens to us. The division can be unclear at times, as in the case of breathing, because we can both feel that we're consciously doing it and that it's something that happens to or through us. Regardless, voluntary and involuntary are seemingly contrasting categories that are mutually dependent because I can't say that I've done something unless there are contrasting acts that I consider of someone else's doing. This is key to understanding what Hindus and Buddhists mean by karma, which, as I mentioned before, simply means "of your own doing." If something unfortunate happens to you, they'll say it's your karma, but that just means that what happens to you occurs according to your own actions. People often misunderstand karma in a superstitious way, as if to say that people are being systematically punished for former misdeeds, but that's not what it means. Karma simply means that you did your accident, just as when you do seemingly involuntary actions such as growing your hair or digesting your dinner.

Now, if you restrict yourself only to what you consider to be voluntary functions, then there seems to be a clear divide between what you did and didn't do. However, when your conception of yourself includes involuntary activities, then others become your others, and involuntary happenings become your deeds. That's rather interesting. As a result of that, you may feel that you really don't do anything at all—for example, that you are in a completely deterministic universe in which everything happens to you, and what some would call voluntary decisions and deeds merely spring from unconscious mental mechanisms that determine everything and leave you a witness to whatever happens. On the other hand, you might feel that you are doing everything, as if you were God. Rocks fall from cliffs, water remains wet, and fire stays hot, all because of you.

Of course, in a way this latter interpretation is true, because the sun requires your eyes to see its light, and rocks are only hard in relation to the softness of your skin, and the weight of objects depends entirely on a certain musculature. So the way you are evokes the way the world is. You could say that there are certain vibrations way out there undetected somewhere in the universe, but these vibrations cannot be observed or described until they encounter some sensitive system. And, again, the sensitive system of our nervous system is just as much a part of the external world, and the external world is an event of the nervous system. The inside of the box is outside the box; the outside is inside.

It's the same way with what we call solid and what we think of as space. Most of us think that reality is what's solid. We talk about *hard* facts, even brute facts. In this way of thinking, space is sort of this unimportant background, but there's no way to imagine a world that's solid without there being space. To begin with, the edges of the solid would be invisible, and, in fact, there wouldn't be such a thing as edges because an edge is a point of interface between a solid and space. If you remove the space, you remove the solid. And yet we conceive of space as something that isn't there—it's just the place where there aren't any obvious solids. This explains why we become puzzled when mathematicians and physicists speak of space as having properties—*curved* space and *expanding* space, for example. For the average person, that kind of talk is just bunk.

Even if we consider solids as the only reality, we can only do so if we actually investigate solids. If you look under a powerful enough microscope, you'll quickly discover that even the densest piece of steel entails more space than anything else. The distances between molecules, atoms, and subatomic particles are incredibly vast, and even those components can't truly be said to be solid. There's a lot more of what we call *nothing* to all of this than there is anything we could call *something*. So space and solid are just poles—the same as self and other, organism and environment, individual and world. Go thoroughly into any of these, and you'll find the other.

What do you mean when you say that you love yourself? What do you love most in the world? Think about it. Personally, I'd say that I love candy, I love beautiful women, I love steak, I love wine, I love good bread. I also love clear water, I love music, and I love the sun on a beautiful landscape. In this way, if you really try to talk about yourself, you'll realize that you can't. Who you are and what you love about yourself invariably involve things other than yourself—things seemingly external—and this is the flip-flopability between pairs of opposites. In the field of yin, you'll find the birth of yang; in the full development of yang, you get the beginning of yin. One implies the other, and they're always flipping. Flipping is the love that makes the world go 'round.

> { We don't really want to live
> in a world in which everything
> is positive all of the time. }

Let's now contrast the principle of difference with the principle of unity. We know what we mean by *difference* because we know what we mean by *one*. Difference implies unity, and unity implies difference, but what lies beyond them both? What's the connecting field between the poles? What's the magnetic tape that lies between the ones and zeroes? Is there something that underlies both yes and no, life and death, light and darkness? Is it what some people call God?

We're trying to play a game between opposites. The game of chess involves opposite sides of light and dark, and when we play chess we want to win. But if I win, it means that you have to lose. Couldn't we invent a game in which no one loses and everybody wins? Well, we could, but not much would happen and we couldn't truly call it a game. And if we try to play a no-lose game, we find it's impossible—we're just setting ourselves up for an impossible task that will leave everybody feeling frustrated. This is what happens when we want everybody to win or when we want it good all the time. We'd like sunshine every day. But nobody really wants that kind of world. We think we do, or we think we ought to, but we don't really want to live in a world in which everything is positive all of the time.

And if we were to come to the conclusion that nothing makes any difference, that it's just black and white, life and death, and good and evil alternately forever and ever and ever and that we can't do anything to change or improve that, we think we'll just sit around and vegetate and feel sort of sad. No—we still have an itch for something else. We can't put up with that—we want to find a way to get through, a way to find what lies beyond the ordinary contrast of pleasure and pain. We're after the metaphysical bliss beyond everything.

How can we make sense of such a thing? In the various accounts of mystical experience provided throughout the ages, people speak of an intense joy in the sudden realization that the dark and the light constitute a harmony. The two are not discordant. I once met an elderly lady who was involved in an accident in an elevator. Her leg was crushed. It took the rescue crew nearly half an hour to free it, and during that time the woman said she had the most extraordinary experience, one in which she realized that there wasn't a single grain of dust in the entire universe out of place.

From a strictly philosophical and logical point of view, it doesn't mean anything to say that everything is good or everything is happy and harmonious. It's the same thing as saying that everything is everything. But anyone who has experienced cosmic consciousness will know that those are not idle words. You can actually experience the positive and the negative—the yes and the no—singing and constituting each other and swinging together in a fantastic dance, and a radiance flows out of the white light while the black outline pulls back, and that withdrawal seems to pull aside a veil to show the white. Did the veil draw back so that the light could shine, or did the light push away the veil?

When we play a game, there's a concept of being a good sport. What that means is that you can be a good loser—that you can play the lose game with the same enthusiasm as when you win. And what you look for in a good opponent is someone who will give you a good run, someone who will win every so often and push you to try harder and keep yourself on top. But if you find that you're always the one who comes out slightly more on top, even that gets boring after a while—it has to be more even to prove interesting. So maybe over the course of a year, you average out—your partner is ahead for six months, but then you pull ahead again once more. And then maybe your partner wins for even longer, which means you'll have to come back and catch up and win for an even greater amount of time, but if you get too far ahead again, the game becomes boring once more.

You can't maintain consciousness without contrast. That's why people go on adventures, take risks, and do all sorts of absolutely foolish things—skydiving, racing cars, and even starting wars. They want to see what happens. Of course, some people are more cautious. For them, life is like a fire, and the whole point is to keep it burning for as long as possible. There are two types of pipe smokers—people who take enormous puffs and cause the pipe to burn out quickly and people who take little puffs here and there so that the pipe lasts for a long time. Some people love a quick, enormous flash; others love a long, slow glow. Who's right? Who's left?

You can take it either way. One goes off with a whimper; another one goes off with a bang. The morning glory blooms so briefly; the giant pine lives for more than a thousand years. A fruit fly lives but a couple of hours; a tortoise may live for hundreds of years. But from their own point of view, maybe they both live the same amount of time. From your point of view, it's always the same. A rich person might think it terrible to be poor, but a person born in poverty might not consider it to be so unusual.

It all comes out the same in the end. It balances out, and we wouldn't want it any other way. You can't have the positive without the negative, and if you want one, you'll have to take the other. And if you think this is a lousy deal, then I invite you to explore what deal you'd prefer. Suggest a better arrangement. I think you'll find that what you come up with won't actually be what you want—at least not for long. The whole nature of wanting involves contrast. If I served you nothing but chocolate eclairs with honey and champagne every day for breakfast, you'd quickly get sick of them. It would be the same thing if you had a harem and had to keep it up constantly, day and night.

If you really go into the problem of life, you'll find it's precisely the way you want it to be. Superficially, things might not look the way you want them to look, and you might want to change them right away, but life is like sleeping on a hard bed. You lie on your left side until you can't stand it, so you turn over on your right, but you eventually get tired of that, so you turn over on your left again. Maybe you try sleeping on your back for a while until that gets too rough and you lie over on your tummy, and then you switch back to your back, and then your tummy, and then your right, and then your left. That's essentially what we're all doing. A bed that is always comfortable would be meaningless because we'd never know what comfortable is.

So here's the puzzle. It has two sides. Side one: I can never beat the game of opposites, and I can never have more positive than negative. Side two: I wouldn't want it any other way because I can't imagine how to improve the game, and involved in this puzzle is the sudden and curious deflation in which I feel out of sorts because there's no impression I can make on anything. But if I try to find this person—this *I* who wanted to interfere and be challenged and is currently put out—I can't find them. I look, but I cannot locate a *myself* as opposed to *they* or *it* because I can never have one without the others.

That deflated, frustrated feeling is simply the realization that there is no such thing as a separate I. If you don't want to feel that truth, you will resist it, but if you're open to that experience, the logic of opposites in the game of black and white will lead you to the ineluctable conclusion that you have no separate self apart from everything you call other.

No Escape

We aren't who we think we are. We aren't a separate self that's trapped inside this bag of skin. We are, instead, the entire thing—the whole vibration system, the undulation, the very pulsation we call existence. That's us, vibrating out in infinite ways.

Now, when some people see this, it can be a little disappointing. They ask, "Is that all?" They can't exactly put their finger on what they were expecting—they just know that they wanted something a little more, maybe a surprise of some sort. When we look at the universe for that surprise—for that little extra something that will give it meaning—we're looking for the wrong thing. The meaning of it isn't separate from the thing itself. It isn't something external that is apart, away, or different. In other words, the meaning of the dance is the dance itself, but to understand that you have to dance—you have to swing.

A Zen student complained to the master that it was hot. "How do we escape the heat?" the student asked. The master replied, "You should go where it is neither hot nor cold." And the student asked, "Where's that?" The master answered, "In the summer, we sweat; in the winter, we shiver." In contrast, in Shakespeare's *Richard II*, Gaunt tells his son—who is about to be banished—"All places that the eye of heaven visits are to a wise man ports and happy havens. Teach thy necessity to reason thus; there is no virtue like necessity. Think not the king did banish thee, but thou the king. . . . Go, say I sent thee forth to purchase honor and not the king exiled thee." But his son—Henry Bolingbroke, the future King Henry IV—doesn't buy it. He says, "O, who can hold a fire in his hand by thinking on the frosty Caucasus? Or cloy the hungry edge of appetite by bare imagination of a feast? Or wallow naked in December snow by thinking on fantastic summer's heat? O, no! The apprehension of the good gives but the greater feeling to the worse."

That's why the Zen master says to swing with it. When it's hot, eat curry; when it's cold, drink ice water. Roll with the punches, just as they do in judo. The colder you try to make it, the hotter it will get. There's nothing you can do to ensure that you have everything you want all the time. You can't simply transform your consciousness into something that remains in a state of pleasure, bliss, or ecstasy.

What happens when you are finally convinced that there is nowhere else to be but now? What happens when you realize that it is impossible to be anywhere else, to be conscious of anything else except what is present, and that there is absolutely no trickery you can play on your mind—whether it be iron-forged discipline, self-hypnosis, or some other form of hocus-pocus—to bring about enlightenment, satori, profound illumination, cosmic consciousness, or whatever else you want to call it? It will always be that the person who needs to be transformed is the one attempting to enact the transforming. It's like trying to pull yourself up by your own bootstraps, biting your own teeth, looking into your own eyes without a mirror, or putting legs on a snake. It can't be done.

It can be discouraging to face this fact, even depressing, but there's nothing to do about that, either. If you're depressed, that's simply the you of the present moment. You can try to escape that with some form of distraction, but all you'd be doing is covering up dirt with paint. So, if you feel let down, meaningless, or depressed by the whole thing, and you also understand that there's nothing you can do about it, what happens?

*{ You can only handle tomorrow
if you don't take it seriously. }*

You simply watch what happens. I don't mean that you simply watch your depressed state happening but everything else, too. There's your breath moving in and out and being still, there's what your eyes see and what your ears hear, there's a whole world happening all around and through you. You might not know what's going to happen next, and you might not know what to make of it anymore, so there's nothing left to do but watch. All escapes lead back to whatever it was you were running away from. You can take all sorts of detours—one detour after another—but eventually they all get shorter and simply bring you back to where you started.

When all of our enterprises and ideals and aspirations meet with the sort of defeat I'm describing, we find ourselves quite naturally—and not in an affected or forced way—in the contemplative state. In that state, we just watch whatever it is that's going on. And when thoughts come up, we understand that the thoughts themselves are futile—at least as far as changing anything is concerned—because believing and following those thoughts is like trying to sweep dust from the stairs with bamboo shadows.

Watch your thoughts in the same way you might notice the ticking of a clock, or birds chattering outside, or water dropping from a leaky faucet. All of that is part of what's going on. Life continues to do its thing. Just watch.

Because the thoughts are just chatter, they'll eventually go away. The past disappears because we know it's just a memory, and the future disappears because it hasn't happened—it's just a thought. Tomorrow never comes.

There is no tomorrow. And if you don't realize that there's no tomorrow, it's useless to make plans for it. But if you do realize that tomorrow isn't coming, then maybe plans will be of some use to you because you can actually enjoy the result of your plans if they happen to work out. You can only handle tomorrow if you don't take it seriously.

Some people—especially people involved with Buddhism, yoga, mysticism, and so on—speak of this in terms of getting rid of ego. And the great snare for anyone who goes into the spiritual disciplines is making a project of getting rid of their ego. They come home from retreats and brag about how much they suffered, how long they sat in meditation, how much pain they went through, and they're terribly proud of the whole thing. What absolute bores. This kind of spiritual braggadocio is nothing more than blowing up and inflating the ego even more to a colossal degree. It's the ambition of the ego to be egoless, so don't be beguiled by this kind of thing.

The ego cannot get rid of itself. It's actually impossible. And when you really examine the situation, all of those spiritual disciplines people undertake to get rid of their ego have in their underlying design the means to persuade you that it can't be done, and not merely in a theoretical way. They are designed to help you actually realize that you can no more get rid of your ego than you can put out a fire with more fire.

A truly egotistic person will be less egotistic than someone who's trying to be self-effacing. And it isn't actually that selfish to come out and tell the truth about what you want—for example, when someone is tired of your company and simply says so: "Sorry, but I don't want to be around anybody right now." We call that selfish, but that kind of selfishness isn't really selfish because with that kind of person you always know where you stand. You will never feel like an imposition on such a person, and that makes for a very comfortable relationship.

You owe it to other people to be just as egotistic as you actually are. When it's time to be selfish, be selfish. If someone asks you for help and you feel like you just have to help them and you come out with your good intentions and make promises of one kind or the other, but you actually don't mean it, then that's much worse. You'll just let them down even more. If you don't want to help or you're feeling too lazy or you'd just rather not, then say so. You shouldn't feel ashamed of saying no because you're going to end up saying no in the end, so you might as well do so up front. Don't tell them you have to think it over if that's your way of saying no. Just tell the truth.

People are always fouling each other up in this way. It's important to be just as egotistic as you are because the ambition to be less egotistic than you are is an insidious form of egotism. There's nothing more reprehensible than the ambition to be a saint.

For this reason, I have nothing against gurus who put people through all sorts of complicated obstacle races. Those people asked for it. And they wouldn't respect the guru in the first place unless the guru made things difficult for them. Anyone who goes to a psychiatrist should have their head examined. Let me emphasize this point: You are responsible. When you go to a guru, you are the one giving the guru the authority to take charge of your spiritual development. In time, the guru will show you that the authority has always been yours, but the guru can't do that just by talking, and so you'll find yourself in all sorts of logical binds and ordeals designed to make you feel miserable. And the guru will keep turning it up until you eventually find out that you're the one who's doing it.

But who is the one who finds that out? In the Euclidean system, a point is something that has position but no magnitude, which is kind of absurd. In mathematics today, we don't define a point at all; we just say that it's a limit of size, which is more useful. So that's what I mean by the *you who finds out*. We don't have to define it further because then we get into whether the you is immortal or not, eternal or not, separate or not, and so on. All of that is just silly.

When I say *I know* or *I do*, it doesn't mean that there is an agent of knowing or a doer of deeds. When I say *I say*, it just means that the saying is coming from somewhere over here, as distinct as from somewhere over there. There is no disjunction between the I and the saying—I am what I say because the saying is the act. This is I while I say it. And it's like that with the rest of the body—*I'm heading, I'm hearting, I'm stomaching, I'm boning, I'm breathing*—all of that is the I while it's happening. It's all a process. It's all wiggles.

The I that supposedly lives in the brain—the mythical soul inhabiting this body—is fictitious. It's just a social convention, much like the equator or a measure of temperature. It can't do anything; it's just that the thought that it can do something gets our psychic processes spinning around.

The only thing you can do is let it happen. Whatever's going on, let it happen. And you're not even *letting* it happen, because how could you stop it from doing so? Even if you were to try to stop it, that effort would be part of the happening. And when you discover that there's nothing left to do but let it happen, you suddenly realize that you are what happens. You're not what's limited to what's inside your skull. You are the wind blowing outside, the cars running down the road, the sun shining, the rattle of human existence. There is no reality that is apart from you.

When you recognize that, don't try to hold on to it. Let it go. Don't make a note of it; don't try to remember it—just see what happens next. Go on. The moment is always new, always fresh, no matter what's going on. Don't try to fix it into any mold; don't call it satori. See, satori is something to keep. Don't keep anything. You can't anyway—it's like pouring water into a bottomless bucket. Let the water flow and flow.

As you let go and go on, you'll see that something is coming toward you all the time. You don't know what it is, and you don't know what's going to happen next, so just watch. You're always right here when it happens—right at the critical moment, which is always this moment. There's no script. There's no use in worrying about whether or not this is what you're supposed to be doing or whether you're right or wrong. The only way there's a script is if you insist on making someone else's script your own. And whatever is coming isn't coming from somewhere or someone else—it's coming from you. The spontaneous arising is you. There isn't any you besides it.

As you well know, the most pleasurable things in life almost always happen unexpectedly. They aren't contrived. When I take students with me to Japan, the first thing I tell them is that we won't be going on a scheduled tour. Most scheduled trips end up being a big disappointment because there's a buildup of expectation. And when traveling in foreign countries, most people only see what they're supposed to see—the Taj Mahal in India, for example—and they go according to plan, because that's what they're supposed to do, and they take pictures with these little black boxes that are devices for capturing experience—click, click, click—and they never actually see anything. They're always looking through the aperture, making sure the picture is just right, and it's an absolute drag. You may have had the opportunity of a lifetime to be at the miraculous Taj Mahal and experience all that it has to offer, and instead you waste your time taking photographs in an effort to preserve a contrived memory. Click.

*{ An essential principle of swinging
and the pursuit of material pleasure
is the unscheduled life. }*

In the United States, we say, "Just follow your nose." In Japan, they say, "Follow your feet," because Japan is easy to wander around in—they have these narrow streets, funny courtyards, and all sorts of curly places for effective wandering. You're not allowed to walk around like that in this country, and if you try to do so in a so-called nice part of town the police will be sure to stop you. Where are you going? Nowhere particular. Well, that's a suspicious thing to be doing, but thankfully you can still do so in Japan. You can take a side turn and not have the faintest idea where you're going, and suddenly you find yourself in the most amazing garden, or in a funny little restaurant that serves the most unusual food, or a bar where they offer you broiled sea snails and there's only room inside for two people to sit, or a shop that sells rare pottery, and even though the shopkeeper can't speak a word of English, he brings out tea for you and shows you the utmost courtesy. These aren't experiences on anyone's itinerary. You only make these discoveries by following your feet.

Of course, for the convenience of other people, some schedule is necessary. That being said, an essential principle of swinging and the pursuit of material pleasure is the unscheduled life. It's okay to have a rough schedule as long as you don't get uptight about it. Just as the skeleton is a framework for the flesh, a schedule is simply a set of bones for wiggles. We need some bones, after all, or else everybody would be too gooey. But that doesn't mean you need to take your bones seriously. Always allow for the unexpected. This is true at the level of the most simple sensuous pleasures as well as the level of the highest mystical experiences.

5

What Is So
of Itself

The *Kena Upanishad* says that Brahman can only be known by those who know it not. Matthew 16 says, "For whosoever will save his life shall lose it." Countless other texts tell us that the highest knowledge isn't knowledge at all. Mystical literature is full of these types of paradoxes. Cosmic consciousness is what arises of itself when you see that nothing arises at all except that which arises of itself.

In other words, life isn't something on the one hand happening to you on the other, or something that's being done by you to it. The whole thing—you and life—is a spontaneous occurrence. In Chinese, the word for *spontaneous* and the word for *nature* are the same—translated into English: "what is so of itself." You can't preconceive of the spontaneous; you can't fake it and merely imitate what you think is spontaneous by going against social convention. That's just acting out the obverse of convention, which means you're just as conditioned by convention as ever. The truly spontaneous can only happen of itself, and you cannot arrange it.

Does that mean to just take things as they come? To just live day to day? A person who asks such questions doesn't know what it means to take things as they come. They have a concept of what it means to live day to day, moment to moment, but it's still just a concept. They think perhaps that ordinary people are full of plans and schemes and anxiety, and therefore the way to be is the exact opposite of that. That's the same as fake spontaneity because taking things as they come doesn't mean that you imitate a placid attitude or put on some other kind of act.

In the same way, people have lots of preconceived notions about mystics, Buddhas, sages, and so on. They often imagine them as having no emotions. When a Zen master gets angry, they get so angry that the room rattles. The difference is that when the anger has passed, it's over—it's gone. It's the same way with children. They can flare up and scream, but then the whole thing vanishes. People think that holy people should have more control over themselves, show little emotion, and be completely serene and placid in all circumstances. Rubbish. Such people would prefer a stone Buddha to a living one. They'd bang away at a saint and see how long it takes them to scream, but of course a saint isn't supposed to scream. ("You didn't scream—you win!") It doesn't make much difference, of course, because a saint like that might as well be dead. That's simply a test of insensitivity. There's no way of saying what the enlightened state is like. There's no stereotype. Anyone who has ever tried to write it down always ends up saying that it's ineffable, that what they're trying to describe isn't really coming across.

When it comes to just taking things as they come, most people think in terms of waking up, eating breakfast, brushing their teeth, maybe taking a shower or looking out the window for a while, putting on clothes, getting on a bus, and seeing what happens after that, but that's not it. When you are in the state I'm referring to, everything in that sequence of ordinary, everyday events is an absolutely weird, magical process that is the entire point of the whole universe, and when you look at everybody else rushing around with their wild, searching eyes and their striving and madness, you feel sorry for them. You don't feel angry at them; you just feel sorry because they don't realize that whatever it is that's going on is it. This is where's it's all going; this is where it all comes from. The alpha and the omega are now.

Spontaneity and the Unborn Mind

For the most part, we're very controlled when it comes to social intercourse. Our conversations typically go along in an expected, linear pattern, and if somebody suddenly changes the subject, it creates a small social crisis. So according to the rules, if we don't want to be viewed as a crazy person who thinks associatively (instead of logically and in a linear fashion), we wait for a pause in the conversation and precede our comments with something like "Excuse me for changing the subject, but . . ." That indicates an adherence to expectations.

But what happens if we change the rules? What if we tell a group of conversing people to say anything that comes into their heads? Watch what occurs if you tell people to free-associate—they suddenly go blank. Something warns them to not move, to not speak, because they can't trust themselves. To help with this, a psychoanalyst will ask you about your dreams, because talking about your dreams is a way of kidding yourself and making statements for which you know you won't be held responsible. You can say something about yourself without admitting that you're saying anything about yourself. See, you already did your free-associating in the dream. The dream was an associative process of thinking rather than a logical one, and you can describe it freely now because it is safely past—it's not happening in the moment.

It's a lot easier to free-associate by drawing pictures. There's not a lot of consequence for drawing a lot of meaningless stuff. But you have to coax people to free-associate with language because words are tremendously powerful in the social scene. People can be blown to pieces with words in nothing flat. Say the wrong word, and everybody blushes—just like that I can produce a complete physiological reaction with nothing but words. For that reason, it's dangerous to get away from the order of words and communicate with people in an unstructured way. But if we all played along and didn't withdraw and realized that it's only words and became curious about the results, then the group as a whole would begin to feel at ease. We'd start to understand that we can trust ourselves to behave in non-egocentric ways without harming others, without creating murder and mayhem and bloodshed, without stealing people's things, and that there's actually a possibility that we could do so and love each other. In fact, this has been done in some spiritual circles for a long time—among Pentecostals, for example.

The koan is a game of challenge and response in which stopping and thinking about a particular situation means that you lose and you're out. You can try again, but you never really know what the situation you're about to respond to is going to be. For example, once upon a time a Zen master posed a particular question to one of his students. The student gave an answer, and the master accepted it. However, after the student left, the master's assistant expressed doubt as to whether or not the student really understood the point, so the master asked the student to return the next day. The student came back, the master asked the same question as the day before, and the student responded in exactly the same way. "No, no, no," said the master. "That's wrong." The student was confused. "But yesterday you said that answer was correct." And the master replied, "I know. Yesterday it was correct, but today it's wrong."

Every situation is different. Things are always changing. The point is to respond in a way that is appropriate to the field of forces as it is right now. And you cannot tell what the field of forces is like by using your intellect, by using analysis, or by any process of conscious criticism. Your body knows. Your brain can also know, but not through conscious attention and the formulation of words. Your brain is capable of finding out, but if you don't trust it, you will fumble along and do silly things, and you have been habituated to not trust your brain.

But it won't work to try to behave spontaneously. That's what you see when people think they're going to paint spontaneously, they're going to make spontaneous noises with a musical instrument, they're going to dance spontaneously, they're going to have nonplays on the stage, or they're going to host happenings where anything goes. By and large, most of these experiments are colossal failures and are completely boring, and it's perfectly understandable why. They're being done by people who don't truly trust themselves. Trusting yourself is actually a kind of discipline.

You can't simply be a great comedian. It's not simply a matter of memorizing jokes or emulating the great comedians of the past or being a good actor who goes off a funny script written by a genius. The whole point of comedy is the element of surprise—the unforeseen joke that nobody expected. That's what really gets people laughing. The ability to pull this off is something you either have or don't have, and to make it even more unique you must do so in a way that not even you yourself know what's coming. The real comedian interacts with the audience in an unstructured situation and pulls in the gags at will as if they were simply ad-libbed. That's someone working with genuine intelligence, with genuine trust.

Similarly, writing poetry is a lot of work. It takes hours and hours to get the melody and beauty of words just right. But it's like polishing a gem—you had to have something worthwhile in the first place. It's not just in the polishing; it's in the gem. Discovering that gem requires trust in your inherent and original intelligence.

This is what the great Zen teacher Bankei called your unborn mind.[1] It's the mind that isn't individualized—it's not the ego. Bankei once said it's the unborn mind at work when you hear something say "caw" and you know right away that it's a crow. He was once heckled by a priest who was standing at the back of the crowd who said, "I don't understand a word you're saying," and Bankei said, "Come closer—I'll explain it to you." The priest moved in a little ways, and Bankei said, "Come closer, even closer," and the man came close to Bankei—right up on the platform with him. Then Bankei said, "Good. How well you understand me!"

In another story, someone asked the master Nanquan about a certain goose. "I heard that there was once a man who grew a goose in a bottle. Eventually it became so large that it couldn't get out. Now, the man didn't want to hurt the goose, and he didn't want to break the bottle. How does he get the goose out?" Nanquan listened and then changed the subject. The questioner got up to leave, and just as he placed his hand on the door, Nanquan shouted, "The goose is out!"

If I say "Hello" to you, and you say "Hello" back to me, you just do it. You don't have to stop to think about it. You don't wonder what mischief I'm up to—you simply respond. Now, you might argue that you do so out of habit, and it is true that we often give conditioned responses that have been fed to us at some point, but we saw quite clearly that this sort of thing doesn't work for the comedian. A comedian needs to access something that goes well beyond habit. It's the same when you find yourself in a crisis and you just spontaneously act with intelligence when there is absolutely no time to go over options and think through various decisions. Your own being steps in and comes to your aid.

Again, this isn't a question of something we ought to do. It's not that we need to have faith in ourselves because it is virtuous to do so or because it means that we are psychologically integrated (and hopefully more psychologically integrated than the people we know). It's not like that at all. In truth, you can't avoid it; you do it all the time. It's only when it comes to your attention that it becomes a problem. When it doesn't come to your attention, you are functioning intelligently without thinking at all, but when you see it happening you think better of it and say, "I probably shouldn't do that."

{ *The only way to let go is to remember that you can't hold on.* }

It's like working for a certain type of boss—the kind you should never ask for advice. Everything goes fine if you simply do your job, but the minute you take your work to them and ask their opinion about what you're doing, they'll hold everything up while they think about it. They can't make up their mind. That's why you shouldn't ask—just go ahead and do your job. You'll save everybody a lot of time and maybe prevent your boss from having ulcers. In the same way, some people always want to know whether a certain action is legal or not, and the best advice is usually to go ahead and do it without asking. There's a saying in Zen that goes something like "Officially, not even a needle is permitted to pass. Unofficially, a carriage and six horses can get through." If the law isn't directly challenged and the authorities asked to make a decision about it, you can probably get away with it.

You can trust in your own organic skill and intelligence. Really, you can't avoid it. If you try to avoid it and tell yourself that you can't trust yourself, then it follows that the very idea that you cannot trust yourself is untrustworthy. After all, it's one of your ideas. If you believe that you can't trust your brain, how can you trust whatever logic it is that underlies that belief? Finally, it does no good to say that you're going to let go and finally trust the field of forces in which you live. Don't do it that way. Instead, remember that you can't hold on. The only way to let go is to remember that you can't hold on. There's nothing to hold on to and no one to hold it. It's all one system, one energy.

Relaxation, Religion, and Rituals

Everything around us is completely magical. Some imaginative people are conscious of this, and they show it by the way they act and whatever they surround themselves with. Notice that there are some people with whom you have either great accord or great fear because they aren't ordinary people—they have imagination; they have an atmosphere of magic. And they're not hiding under an attempt to conform to the ideal of being ordinary. Some artists are like this, as well as what I call *relaxed people*. Relaxed society is a wonderful class of people. They're not on edge all the time. Some people are always edgy, and you end up feeling that your presence is messy or disturbing to them.

Relaxed people, on the other hand, have what in Arabic is called *barakah*, which translates to something like "divine grace." An old frying pan with long years of use is just perfect the way it is—that's barakah. We can try to reproduce that by finding some scientific process for artificially antiquing things—for putting a patina on bronze in five minutes, say, or preaging wine—but those attempts rarely work. And it's all phony because barakah only comes through the process of growth. People don't want to wait, but the whole thing is in the waiting. I don't mean the virtue of patience; I mean waiting when there's nothing to do but wait. When you see that there's nothing to do but wait, that's when it happens. It can't be hurried. The minute you try to hurry the process, that very attempt is what will stop it from happening. The miracle is happening all the time, but you can't see it when you're trying to get it, and you see it even less when you're trying to get it fast.

You are going to be you—you're going to be the same slob you've always been. You can't change that. All of your good resolutions are just bombast. But when you see that, you begin to be real and relax. Your weakness is actually your strength. The strong thing isn't your big ego and your big will—it's your sloppiness, your weakness, your foolish side.

Gorgeous things are happening all of the time by themselves. The most astounding insights and truest pleasures are in the most trivial of everyday affairs. This is what all of those Zen stories are about. A monk sweeps the courtyard, and a small piece of broken tile hits the bamboo and pop! The monk sees the secret of the entire universe in that one sound. It can happen like that with anything—light through a dewdrop or the sound of a bell. Any point can be a taking-off point.

There's a principle I referred to earlier that the Japanese call jijimuge. Looking at this word in pieces, *ji* refers to any experience you could identify as a thing or event, and the doubling of *ji* here means "between thing/event and thing/event." *Mu* means "no," and *ge* means "barrier" or "obstruction," so to put the whole principle in other words: "Every event implies all others." When you pick up one link of a chain, the rest of the chain comes along with it. When you pick up one thing/event, the whole universe comes along with it. There are no separate things—it's all a single, unified process that cannot truly be divided into voluntary and involuntary, I and you, or free and determined, because all of it is the big happening. All of those categories are merely ideas about it, and we can abandon all of that because it's just a net designed for catching water.

When you stop running around trying to capture pleasure, there it is. And you don't have to feel anxious anymore about it sticking around. You don't have to worry about that anymore, because you know that if you do worry, you'll simply shoo it away. What a tremendous relief! You no longer have to bother with whether the pleasure will stick around or whether you'll lose your insight or whether your satori will take wing and fly off with the bats. The more you let go of it, the more it stays. And even your worry about making sure you let go of it is just a hang-up.

The Chinese master Yoka Daishi put it this way: You cannot take hold of it, you cannot get rid of it, and in not being able to get it, you get it. When you are silent, it speaks, and when you speak, it is silent. The great gate is wide open, and nobody obstructs it.

There are a number of reasons why I don't like to argue with anybody about their religion, mostly because everybody's religion is the same thing as their life. Now, their life might be a weird life, but speaking from the Hindu point of view, that's just their trip this time around. In the world of illusion, the Godhead plays all the parts—the villains as well as the heroes, the fools as well as the sages, and the sinners as well as the saints. So I'm not out to convert anybody or win souls, because that's like telling a group of pigs that they should all be cows, or telling a giraffe that its neck is too long, or going up to an elephant and complaining about its weight.

I suppose most of you are familiar with the works of Krishnamurti. You'll find a lot in common with what he teaches and what I do, although I think he's more of a purist in that he takes a rather negative attitude toward things that are recognizably religious. He sets no store by religious literature, ceremonies, meditation, and so forth, and he wouldn't dream of being involved in a ritual, at least no ritual that could be construed as religious in any way.

I do my best to see people for what they are—not for the purposes of trying to classify them and put them in a type of box but to see if it's possible to find the divine in their disguise. Kabir was an Indian mystic and poet who lived in the fifteenth century. He's famous for seeing the beloved—the Godhead—on all sides in every being, and he therefore felt it would be presumptuous to preach or make recommendations to anybody. The Godhead takes countless forms, and Hindu mythology is known for having some nitty-gritty characters. Take Kali, for example. She represents the dark side of yin—the feminine of the feminine, the devouring feminine force that sucks everything into its darkness. Kali is typically shown with fangs, her skin is black, and she carries a scimitar in one hand and a severed head in the other. She's an entirely bloody character, and yet she's the mother of the universe. There are Kalis all around us. We want to say, "Kali's not so bad—she has her good side after all," but that's not the thing. The thing is to see her frightening side itself as an aspect of the divine. If we can do that, we can refrain from asking her to change or improve.

{ The mystery of life is not a problem to be solved but a reality to be experienced. }

I know it's tough to do that. Personally, I have immense distaste for the lunatic fringe of Protestantism—Jehovah's Witnesses, say, or a Southern Baptist of the Billy Graham type. I don't understand them. I wonder what the real kick in that is—what are they really doing? What pleasure do they get out of it? How can the Godhead be playing that game? It's a mysterious business. And I try to look at it as a mystery, because that's a lot better than telling them to cease and desist all of those religious gimmicks and vanity. Most religious gimmicks are just vanity from my point of view, but I think of what William Blake said: "The fool who persists in his folly will become wise." For this reason, I consider the possibility that even foolish religions are ways of realization—the more far out you get from realization, the closer to it you come because the path is a circle.

For the most part, we look at religion or spirituality and wonder what it can do for us. If I pray in such and such a way or meditate or practice yoga, what can I get out of it? What magic will it help me perform? But we don't have to do that. Instead, we could approach them in the same way as we do art. We don't look at a painting or sculpture and wonder what it will do for us; we don't listen to music because we think it offers a particular benefit. We appreciate art in all of its forms simply because we enjoy it—it's fun and beautiful. And that makes us want more. If we take this attitude toward any practice that's designated as religious, we can enjoy it as a way of expressing exuberance, delight, a sense of wonder, and an appreciation of the magic of being.

As various people have said, the mystery of life is not a problem to be solved but a reality to be experienced. People who try to explain mysteries are the ones who end up destroying them, and to destroy mysteries is to destroy life. May we all remain mysterious to one another.

Despite what Krishnamurti says, I think we would be greatly impoverished if we abandoned meditation, or going to church, or participating in rituals of all sorts. What would happen if we did? Churches would become museums, the holy scriptures would be used to start fires, rituals would only live on in funny dances, and we'd be scrubbed clean of all superstition. From an aesthetic point of view, I don't look forward to any of that. Personally, I like magical toys. I don't believe in them in the sense of thinking they will help me in the competitive games of life, but when I see a figure of the Buddha seated on a lotus throne with incense burning in front of him, I feel something glowing, warm, civilizing, humanizing, and at the same time mysterious. It's hard to put my finger on it.

I especially enjoy the images and practices you find in Mahayana Buddhism, which is such an urbane, sophisticated religion. It doesn't pursue you or harass you with preachments; it doesn't make a busybody nuisance of itself. And yet it fosters the arts, compassion, and concern, but not the kind of concern that tries to shove what's supposed to be good for you down your throat. It's roomy. That's why it's called the Mahayana—the Great Vehicle, or the Great Course. It entails so many different ways and practices and isn't overly plagued with officiality.

That's the type of Christianity I like, too, mostly as it's expressed in Roman Catholicism or Eastern Orthodoxy. I don't so much like the scrubbed type of Protestantism, where they've removed the candles and vestments and incense and mystery. They've made it all so rational and essential, and whenever people reduce any religion down to what they call the essentials, they end up getting rid of the important things and keeping the misleading ones. All religions offer a way of salvation or a path of liberation, whatever it may be. The Protestants thought that Catholic rituals and obscure practices were getting in the way of people reaching God directly, and they wanted a more efficient and straight path, as if they were planning to reduce the course of study from ten years to a mere ten weeks. But that made the whole enterprise of religion into something intended to get something else, and that doesn't work. Trying to get God means that you have assumed that you aren't already there. When you don't try, there's a chance you might actually discover that.

What is fascinating about the more inefficient religions is precisely their colorfulness and all of the nonessential things they do. Do you notice that the first thing that efficient religions do is to remove all of the color? So they wear black because color shows dirt, and you have to wash it all the time. See, that's efficiency. But efficiency doesn't matter so much if your religion isn't based in acquisition.

Religion doesn't have to be that way. You could begin from the point of recognition that you are what you are and that you can't actually improve yourself, because trying to do so only gets you more tied up in knots and messed up. You have to recognize that—there's no alternative. Instead, you could just very simply and ingenuously be aware of life without trying to do anything about it. When you let it happen, it begins to show its color. Then you can feel the marvel and magical nature of the world, so whatever you do from there in terms of religious practice is simply an art form like singing or dancing. You don't sing and dance in order to secure yourself. You don't sing and dance so that you can acquire something or earn a reward. You do so simply to express marvelous feelings and live it up.

It's difficult for people to understand how you could be living it up by meditating. On the surface, meditation seems so dull. Sitting still for long periods of time just appears awful. It seems much like when you were a kid and your parents made you sit still when you really wanted to be jumping around, so you resented it. And there are actually types of meditation like that—dervish dancing, for example—if that's more to your temperament. Here's the thing about ordinary, sitting meditation, though—nobody seems to realize that it's supposed to be fun.

It's like what happens when you're sick and you have to lie in bed all day. Everybody else in the world is out going about their business, and you're left at home with almost nothing to do except listen. So you end up hearing all of these funny noises that you normally don't notice—people and animals and birds and other things—and it suddenly occurs to you that what you're hearing is an unheeded symphony of everything that's going on. And then you notice sunlight leaving curious patterns on the walls or the intricate designs the cracks make in the ceiling. You notice all of this because you are in a condition of complete receptivity and passivity, so everything comes to life. Passivity is the root of life—it's the womb from which all creation starts.

In some forms of meditation, you'll be given something to meditate on—for example, a visual image like a chakra or mandala, or a sound that you can hum—although it isn't necessary to do so. You can simply sit there not doing anything (and not trying to do anything) and slowly become aware of everything that's going on because you're not in a hurry and there's nowhere to go. Granted, for some people this isn't easy. You can feel restricted and impatient. However, if you take it easy, you won't feel such restriction. It's like lifting a heavy weight and holding it up—the more you fight against that feeling of tension, the worse it gets. So if your legs hurt while you're meditating or you get truly uncomfortable, it's possible to take a certain attitude wherein the discomfort simply disappears. Then you have this extraordinary feeling that comes from looking at life without having to do anything about it—you can just let it happen with no sense of hurry and with no wish to improve it.

That's why the images of the Buddha always present him as looking blissful. Cats look like this, too, because they can sit for ages and simply watch. You might say it's because they have nothing better to do because we think we're supposed to be constantly improving somehow or doing something beneficial for the world. But hermits who live solitary lives and meditate all of the time are doing an enormous amount for the world, and just the suspicion that people such as that still exist today is marvelous for everybody. The contrast of their presence reveals how the rest of us are so busy raising so much dust. We think we're going somewhere, but we're already there. Meanwhile, all the dust we kick up rushing about everywhere is getting in everybody's nostrils and polluting everything. So to know that there are hermits deep in the forest is like knowing there's a world beyond the dust—a world of streams and flowers that few of us ever see.

If most of us heard of a hidden valley full of streams and flowers, we'd want to open it up to the public and put in a ranger station, toilet facilities, and a picnic ground. It would be even worse if we suspected that somebody was living in that beautiful, flowery valley all alone—we'd call that person a selfish bastard and open it up so that everybody could have a look, destroying the valley in the process.

I live opposite a forest. It's quite large and dense, and it occupies the whole side of one valley. Sometimes I think it would be fun to explore it, but then I decide not to because I don't want to disturb it. You never see people over there—there's just an old she-goat who comes out every so often to climb on top of a big rock, and there are also birds, deer, skunk, rabbits, and so on. I think it's best to leave that forest alone. When we take a meditative, hands-off approach to life, it benefits other people in the same way as an untouched forest benefits people. It's essential to our sanity. We need areas of life that aren't interfered with.

So that's the passive side of exuberant religion—the meditative approach. The other side, of course, has more to do with music, dancing, and rituals of all sorts. Take the Japanese tea ceremony, for example. It's not considered magic, nobody is really expecting to get anything out of it, and it's purely a secular ritual for drinking tea together. In actuality, it's a Zen Buddhist ritual that doesn't see any difference between religion and everyday life. It entails the beauty of gesture and primitive vessels, and the ritual is done for no other reason except the serenity of the ritual itself.

There's very little joyous ritual in the United States today. Even the Catholic rituals here feel more like a clowning affair in which people dress up and give money to charity and engage in an abbreviated form of confession. I once attended a midnight mass in New York, and I never saw anything go so fast. There's a story by Alphonse Daudet called "Les trois messes basses" in which a priest and some acolytes rush through the three masses of Christmas in one hell of a hurry because they're all eager to get to dinner. Well, they give themselves such indigestion at the meal that they all die, and their ghosts have to celebrate the masses over and over again for the rest of eternity. This mass was just like that. There was nothing stately about it, there was no rhythm, and there was no sense of dance. They just wanted to get the thing ground out as fast as possible.

Who wants that? That's like using a prayer wheel with an electric motor. Have you ever twirled a prayer wheel? It has a cylinder and a little chain with a weight on the end of it, and on the inside of the wheel are prayers of various sorts, and around and around it goes, much like the earth around the sun. But it's not that easy to twirl—there's a trick to it. You don't want the chain to get loose and drop the weight down, so you have to keep the rhythm going, but you can't rush it—you can't be in a hurry. You just twirl and twirl without trying to get anything, like some kind of nut. And you have to be a nut to do it; you have to be at your wits' end. But you don't have to do anything else but twirl that wheel. You don't have to say anything; you don't have to think anything; you don't have to be virtuous; you don't have to believe anything at all. You just spin it, and you can have a ball swinging that thing.

We need to be delivered from utilitarian religion altogether and come to the realization that the highest form of religion is perfectly useless. That's the true nature of play after all—the true nature of the universe. The Godhead, the saints, the angels, and all of those Buddhas sitting serenely in their mandalas—all of them are quite useless. They serve no purpose whatsoever. They're not good for anybody or anything because they don't need to be. And they're not going anywhere because they're already there.

Saving the World

What happens when you don't have some sort of purpose to work out? What happens when you don't have to get someplace directly? You slow down; you wander; you notice things. And that's how you come across the winged path as opposed to the straight. You can just go round and round in circles, just as the planets do around the sun, which is going around something else out there. You can twirl around as we do while holding hands in some religious dances, or exactly as your breath moves around and around, in and out. It doesn't go in and out like a pump; there's a circular flow to it. It goes around and around, just as the world does, just like existence—samsara.

Samsara—the wheel of becoming, the wheel of birth and death, the sorry-go-round (as distinct from a merry-go-round). In Sir Edwin Arnold's poem *The Light of Asia*, he has the Buddha say,

> Ye suffer from yourselves. None else compels,
> None other holds you that ye live and die,
> And whirl upon the wheel, and hug and kiss
> Its spokes of agony,
> Its tire of tears, its nave of nothingness.[2]

You think you're getting somewhere, but you're not. That's why we call it the rat race. Spin the wheel round and round, but what you gain on the roundabout you lose on the swings. There are some people who can take a different sort of attitude toward the wheel of fortune and gamble and spin it just for fun. They're not hung up on the game—they aren't gambling in order to make money. So the mandala is a symbol of the rat race, but transformed.

Have you seen paintings of the Buddhist wheel of life? Up top you have successful people—they're the angels—and down at the bottom are unsuccessful people in purgatorial states of extreme suffering. In between these you have graduated states of miscellaneous humans, frustrated spirits, furious demons, and animals, with gods up on top. The demons and tormented spirits are at the bottom. And everybody is trying to move up, but wherever you are, it's the bottom—you're in your own kind of torment. Even the gods are striving, trying to stay in heaven, because there's nowhere else to go from there but down. Now, it's important to note that you won't find a Buddha on top of this wheel because a Buddha is liberated, and if you're on the wheel, you're stuck. So how do you get off?

> { *For the person who*
> *is a master of pleasure,*
> *everything in life is a ritual.* }

Wherever you are on the wheel is it. Just be there. If you're as low as you can get, you can see that every point on the wheel is the same, and viewing it that way gives you an entirely different picture of the wheel. You start to see that it isn't so much about rotary movement, as about a flow from the center to the circumference, and then again from the circumference to the center—like a flower. And the path of the petal and your wheel suddenly becomes a mandala—a circle divided by petals, a floral shape. Then you can see the wheel is balanced, joyous, and beautifully bejeweled.

That is the transformation of the rat race. If you watch a skilled craftsperson at work—a surgeon, dentist, shoemaker, or potter who thoroughly loves their work—you'll notice their hands, how they caress and dance as they do whatever it is they do. They look ritualistic in their actions, almost as if they're worshipping some form of god, and the action of whatever they're doing is far more important than the final product. They've turned the rat race into a mandala, and you can do so as well, as long as you're not in a hurry and you're not in a hurry because you know there's nowhere to go.

Take delight in all the ordinary things you have to do. It's supposed to be more rewarding to get your work out of the way so that you can go do something else, but the reward is right here. There's no hurry. For the person who is a master of pleasure, everything in life is a ritual. You can realize the great life if you're not looking for it.

My friend Gary Snyder once said that it's impossible for us to go about the business of saving the world unless we realize that it doesn't need saving. The Hindus say that we're headed toward the end of the Kali Yuga—the destructive period of time that comes every four million years or so—and if they're correct, then the ecological disaster we're facing is simply the periodical death of our world system. Seen in that way, there's nothing especially tragic about it. It's just the way things go, much like the individual death we each must face. You might think that viewing things from this point of view would make a person cold or indifferent, but the truth is quite different. If you understand what you're facing and you don't fight what's happening, you're no longer afraid of it, and if you're no longer afraid of it, you can handle it. The preservation of the planet—the preservation of life—is not a frantic duty. It's a pleasure.

Notes

Chapter 1: Going With

1. Pierre Teilhard de Chardin, *Le Phénomène Humain* (Paris, FR: Éditions du Seuil, 1955).

Chapter 2: Civilizing Technology

1. This excerpt is from an Anglican hymn written by Cecil Frances Alexander in 1848, possibly inspired by William Paley's *Natural Theology* (1802), which expounds on earlier arguments of God as designer of the natural world. The verse in question (verse three) is, as Watts suggests, frequently omitted in available versions of the hymn.

2. Buckminster Fuller (1895–1983) was a systems theorist, inventor, and author of more than thirty books. In addition to Watts, Fuller inspired a number of twentieth-century visionaries, including John Cage, Robert Anton Wilson, and Stewart Brand.

3. Another contemporary of Watts, Marshall McLuhan (1911–1980) was a Canadian philosopher who predicted the Internet nearly thirty years before its invention.

4. In this paragraph, Watts paraphrases some of the work of Harry Stack Sullivan (1892–1949) and George Herbert Mead (1863–1931), both psychologists who stressed that an individual can only be understood in the context of their social environment.

5. Jiddu Krishnamurti (1895–1986) was an Indian philosopher whom Watts references a couple of times in this book.

Chapter 3: Money and Materialism

1. Henry Miller (1891–1980) was an American writer. Watts has mentioned this quotation elsewhere (for example, in *The Tao of Philosophy*), although I haven't been able to locate the original source.

2. Robert Theobald (1929–1999), economist and futurist author, was best known for his writings on post-scarcity economics.

Chapter 4: In Praise of Swinging

1. This is Watts's own translation of a haiku by Taigu Ryokan (1758–1831), an eccentric Soto Zen monk.

Chapter 5: What Is So of Itself

1. Bankei Yotaku (1622–1693) was a Rinzai Zen master known for his revolutionary "Unborn Zen," often cited by Watts (for example, in *Out of Your Mind*).

2. This excerpt is from Arnold's book-length narrative poem, published in 1879, describing the life of Gautama Buddha.

About the Author

Born in Chislehurst, UK, in 1915, Alan Watts moved to the United States as a young man and pursued Zen Buddhist training, also earning a master's degree from Seabury-Western Theological Seminary in Evanston, Illinois. After leaving the Episcopal priesthood in 1950, Watts moved to California and taught at the American Academy of Asian Studies in San Francisco, where he eventually became dean and went on to receive an honorary doctorate in divinity from the University of Vermont. He lectured at universities and growth centers around the world for years and went on to author over two dozen books, including *Psychotherapy East & West*, *The Book: On the Taboo Against Knowing Who You Are*, and *The Way of Zen*—one of the first bestselling books on Buddhism. Watts also recorded hundreds of interviews and seminars and wrote countless articles for popular magazines such as *Elle*, *Redbook*, and *Playboy*. He is widely considered to be the West's foremost interpreter of Buddhism, Hinduism, and Taoism. His son, Mark Watts, produced the documentary film *Why Not Now?* and carries on his father's work with the Alan Watts Electronic University.

About Sounds True

Sounds True is a multimedia publisher whose mission is to inspire and support personal transformation and spiritual awakening. Founded in 1985 and located in Boulder, Colorado, we work with many of the leading spiritual teachers, thinkers, healers, and visionary artists of our time. We strive with every title to preserve the essential "living wisdom" of the author or artist. It is our goal to create products that not only provide information to a reader or listener but also embody the quality of a wisdom transmission.

For those seeking genuine transformation, Sounds True is your trusted partner. At SoundsTrue.com you will find a wealth of free resources to support your journey, including exclusive weekly audio interviews, free downloads, interactive learning tools, and other special savings on all our titles.

To learn more, please visit SoundsTrue.com/freegifts or call us toll-free at 800.333.9185.

In loving memory of Beth Skelley, book designer extraordinaire. Her spirit lives on in our books and in our hearts.